Creating a Life

Marie-Louise von Franz, Honorary Patron

**Studies in Jungian Psychology
by Jungian Analysts**

Daryl Sharp, General Editor

Creating a Life

Finding Your Individual Path

JAMES HOLLIS

To Jill and to our children Taryn and Tim, Jonah and Seah, and to our grandchildren Rachel Erin, Nicholas James, and Benjamin Ryan . . . and to the memory of our beloved Ilhasa, "Shadrach," *semper fidelis.*

I want to thank Daryl Sharp and Vicki Cowan of Inner City Books, who have helped me produce six children of another kind.

I wish also to thank all my friends and colleagues at the C.G. Jung Educational Center of Houston, Texas, where creating a life is our daily work.

Canadian Cataloguing in Publication Data

James Hollis, 1940-
Creating a life: finding your individual path

(Studies in Jungian psychology by Jungian analysts; 92)

Includes bibliographical references and index.

ISBN 0-919123-93-7

1. Self-perception.
2. Developmental psychology.
3. Jungian psychology.
I. Title. II. Series.

BF724.85.S43H64 2001   155.2   C00-931989-1

INNER CITY BOOKS
Box 1271, Station Q, Toronto, ON M4T 2P4, Canada

Telephone (416) 927-0355 / FAX (416) 924-1814
Web site: www.innercitybooks.net / E-mail: admin@innercitybooks.net

Honorary Patron: Marie-Louise von Franz.
Publisher and General Editor: Daryl Sharp.
Senior Editor: Victoria Cowan.

INNER CITY BOOKS was founded in 1980 to promote the understanding and practical application of the work of C.G. Jung.

Cover: "Dance of Life," monoprint by Vicki Cowan.

Printed and bound in Canada by University of Toronto Press Incorporated

CONTENTS

See final page for descriptions of other Inner City Books

PART ONE

The Context,
Which Is the Problem, Partly . . .

1
Creating a Life
The Necessity of Personal Myth

The older I get, the more obscure life becomes. I had thought it would be otherwise—clearer and clearer, until the opacity resolved and one saw through the glass darkly into clarity of understanding.

The older I get, the more determined we seem to be. I had thought it would be otherwise—greater and greater freedom through understanding and will, and of course a little luck along the way.

The older I get, the more the rejected past, outlived attitudes and embarrassing history insinuate themselves, albeit in ever-changing forms. I had thought it would be otherwise—breaking free to transcend origins, liberate loved ones, transform fear into freedom.

The older I get, the more the heroic thinking of youth and early adulthood seems naive and delusional. I had thought it would be otherwise—redemption of ancestry, achievement of enduring goals, and the building of the kingdom . . . well, some kingdom anyway.

It is in the mid to late 1940's. A child has been hurt by another who has fled. He stands shaking, crying, in impotent rage. One of the big persons comes over and sprays him with a hose, saying, "Here, this will cool you down." He learns then that he has no right to feel what he feels. He will spend a lifetime alternately seeking to feel what he feels, or splitting off what he feels, or denying that he feels at all.

The older I get, the more it seems that one may only run around the globe in order to return to the place where one began. I had thought it would be otherwise—the farther one got away, the further one got away.

The older I get, the more it seems that the new is but thinly disguised old. I had thought it otherwise—that life would be a series of developmental departures into the ever-new, the ever-different.

The boy is singing "Home on the Range" while swinging on the porch. A big person comes out, yells at him, strikes him and, inside, song switches off, forever. In high school, when he is forced into choir, he opens his mouth to be tested and nothing comes out. His friends roar with laughter; his teacher is enraged at his apparent defiance. He will never sing again, not even in showers.

The older I get, the more devoted I am to human liberation, and the more pessimistic about change. I had thought otherwise—that information meant knowledge, knowledge meant wisdom, that wisdom meant possibility.

The older I get, the more devoted I am to those oppressed, and the more convinced that their economic and spiritual impoverishment will continue. I had thought it otherwise—that humankind was locked into an evolutionary spiral, that progress existed, and that people could live together without hurting each other.

Day after day, the child is held down on the rough concrete basement floor by the big person and the nozzle of an enema is forced into his rectum. He screams with pain as the water distends the cavities. Once he finds mounds of dirt to place in the toilet to prove his worth, his sincerity at the obligated task, but the dirt dissolves, and he is beaten, and then is sodomized by the black nozzle and the red tube and bladder of scalding water. Decades later he stands in the shower and weeps, the only safe place, where tears are indistinguishable from shampoo.

*

The older I get, the more I am haunted by the ghosts, the psychic reflexes, and the summons of the room beneath the floor. I had thought it otherwise—that the future brings release from the past, that one could fully leave that other time, that other place, and be somewhere else.

And yet, I love my life, have been blessed beyond desire and worthiness, and am fully committed to fight the good fight. That child in the basement was left behind years ago, millennia ago, and was replaced with a savvy, cool, driven professional who brooks no nonsense, is impatient with waste and indolence, and has his agendas set out for years in advance.

This book seeks to wrestle with these contradictions. As Jung said:

[The] apparently unendurable conflict is proof of the rightness of your life.
A life without inner contradiction is only half a life, or else a life in the

Beyond which is destined only for angels. But God loves human beings more than angels.[1]

This whole thing, then, this life, is one big contradiction. That much I can understand.

But is not the purpose of therapy precisely to resolve this conflict, untie this paradox, free history from its replicative madness? Are not all those self-help books devoted to the irresistible fantasy of self-cure, villain identification and vilification, and subsequent facile transformation? Are not the talk shows replete with flatulent examples of bad parents, weeping siblings and reconciliation just before the commercial break? Is not the primal fantasy of America the self-made person, the one who breaks ties with the old world, sets off across distant prairies of personality and reinvents identity? Are we not all immigrants in this new land—original, severed from roots and superior to history? And why is it so confusing, so disorienting, when what we reinvent is still chaos, when we still suffer dismay and constantly find ourselves further and further from our homes?

The fundamentalists of all stripes have ready answers for these perplexities. Get right with God—their God, not the one you might encounter on your private road to Damascus. Adopt the right attitude, right conduct, right spiritual practices, and you will enter the kingdom of the blessed. Be a good citizen, avoid excess, pay your dues, expect your reward, and be reassured by your congruence with those around you.

The more you are like the others, the more secure you will feel, yet the more your heart will ache, the more dreams will be troubled and the more your soul will slip off into silences. Finally, one day, you will have forgotten that you have a soul—you will rise, drive through the traffic, arrive at work, and not remember how you got there. Once you reach that condition, there is no further need to think about much or face painful choices. You will have developed enough conditioned reflexes to make it through your life on automatic pilot. Maybe that was the freedom you sought, the release from torturous thought, colliding emotions, and the

---

[1] Jung, *Letters,* vol. 1, p. 375.

burden of growing up. Maybe now you can relax, hang out, wait to die, and stay tuned to the morning news which reassures you that the old saying is correct: *plus ça change, plus la même chose.*

*

Humans have long speculated upon these paradoxes, these mysteries: how to be, what to be, to what end, whether we are really free to choose or whether dark gods control all, and even whether there is any meaning possible in a world which seems so chaotic, so absurd, and ends in personal annihilation. Nonetheless, the chief fantasy of therapy remains, virtually unquestioned in our culture: *Insight brings choice; choice brings change; change brings liberation.* I am not at all sure this is wrong. Indeed I have staked my professional and personal life on this fantasy. I believe it is true because I have experienced it. And yet . . . and yet, everywhere I see the deep patterns reforming, distorting vision, seducing reason and reenacting their old, old story.

Twenty-five centuries ago the Greek imagination played with these questions and came up with as telling a set of metaphors as obtain in contemporary psychology. Primordial forces move, ineluctably, impersonally, implacably, and even the gods must conform. Fate, or *moira,* embodies the world of givens, the world of limitations, the world of cause and effect. Our genetics, our family of origin, our Zeitgeist, the interplay of intergenerational influences—each is part of our fate.

One woman has a tendency to bipolar disorder and cannot hold her life to a constant line; a man has Barrett's esophagus and finds cancer rushing toward him as his years advance; this child, one in every hundred, will become schizophrenic after puberty, no matter what the culture or century of origin. Another child is born in Warsaw in 1936 and rides a cattle car to Sobibor or Maidanek. This is *moira*—not a god, but god-like in its omnipotence. There are children born into the hands of an abused parent who knows only the rule of the fist. Some are thrust into a time and place where an entire gender is oppressed. And, far more subtly, most children are carriers of that greatest of burdens, the unlived life of the parent and the parent's parent. Whatsoever is unaddressed by one generation is rolled over into the next by way of example, admonition or omission. These unconscious, clustered energies, called complexes by Jung, are conveyed by direct experience internalized, or by the transmission of unconscious motifs whose influence may only be seen, if at all, many years later, and often after great suffering.

In the classical imagination the paradox of fate is balanced by the idea of *hybris*(hubris) for which we have no direct translation. It means arrogance at times, a character flaw at others, or sometimes simply the limitation of possible knowledge. Hubris is found in our capacity to convince ourselves that we really know what is going on. It is found in our capacity for self-deception, in the notion that we can choose with impunity, that we are in control, that we have covered all possible angles. Such delusion is a form of magical thinking, whereby we seek to manage existential anxiety through the fantasy of control and domination.

The Greek positing of hubris is paralleled by the Judeo-Christian concept of sin, though they are not the same thing. Etymologically the word sin derives from an archery term which means to miss the mark. As the archer is flawed, as the wind of fate shifts the flight of the arrow, imperfect achievement is virtually inevitable.

A more recalcitrant feature of the human psyche is hinted at by St. Paul when he admits that though he often knew the good, he did not always, or often, choose the good. The Pauline qualification of missing the mark introduces a more sinister dimension to the matter, much closer to that intimated in hubris. Something within us seeks destruction. Hubris involves the extension of human possibility beyond the humanly possible. It involves crossing the line, even when the line is invisible.

Such an encounter with the implacable occurs in that moment when Hector has triumphed over his foe Patroclus. With his dying breath, Patroclus looks up at the mighty Hector and reminds this Trojan hero:

> "Remember it took three of you to kill me.
> A god, a boy, and, last and least, a hero.
> I can hear Death pronounce my name, and yet
> Somehow it sounds like *Hector*.
> And as I close my eyes I see Achilles' face
> With Death's voice coming out of it."
> Saying these things Patroclus died.

And as his soul went through the sand
Hector withdrew his spear and said:
"Perhaps" . . .[2]

At the moment of his greatest triumph, Hector is reminded that he is overweening, that his arrogance will activate the forces of the cosmos to bring him to his knees. He has a final appointment with Achilles, with death, and with the restoration of the balance.

In addition, the classical imagination identified a condition they called *hamartia,* which has been translated as "the tragic flaw," but which I prefer to define as "wounded vision." Each protagonist believed that he or she understood enough to make proper choices, yet their vision was distorted by personal, familial and cultural history, dynamically at work in what we later called the unconscious.

How can one choose clearly, prudently, when the lens through which one sees the world is itself provisional and distorting? How could one not choose wrongly when one cannot see anything but through such a lens? The sum of one's choices become a body of fate even though one is ostensibly free to choose otherwise. Such a *karma* is heavy freight for the spirit, and an inherited burden for the next generation. The Oedipus of Thebes believes his reputation, that he is the wisest man of Thebes; the Oedipus of Colonus believes himself the lowliest of creatures. A world of suffering, expiation and possible enlargement lies between those two cities of the soul.

Greek tragedy was a therapy of history long before therapy as we know it was invented. When we recall that the word therapy comes from the Greek *therapeuein,* meaning to pay attention or to listen to, then we understand that the tragic vision was the therapy of both the protagonist and the *Polis* as well. In his *Poetics* Aristotle traces the interstices of private and public wounding, and how the redemption of one helps the healing of the other. We moderns would do well to remember that the pathology of the *Polis* is the sum of the unattended complexes of its members, and that the work of personal therapy brings the gift of healing to the body politic as well. What has been denied in the individual will

---

[2] Homer, *War Songs,* p. 171.

breed monsters in the tribe, as ancient literature shows.

The classical imagination embodied the forces which seem to hold the universe in a balanced dynamic. *Dike*, or justice, is one such restorative power whose image of balanced scales is universally recognized. *Sophrosyne*, meaning moderated balance, is another such power, which brings the great circle round to its point of origin. Exult, Hector, for this brief moment, before those invisible powers move gods, move history, move you to another, unintended appointment.

Not only did the classical imagination body forth an heroic image, shadowed always by the powers of death, finitude and restoration, it also articulated the tragic vision. The tragic vision is neither morbid nor negative; it is a statement about the interlocking powers of fate and hubris and how they collide in a person to form character. The tragic figure can curse the gods, malign fate, but he also knows that he has brought the roof down on his head by his own choices. Through suffering he is brought to his knees, his hubris rebuked, his human place restored.

Presume not. The only good life is the short life, before one suffers catastrophic loss. The only wise person is he who knows he knows not. Fear God and go in humility. In Adam's Fall, sinned all. Such admonitions ripple throughout the wisdom literature of the ancient world. Why so much admonition, why the steady drumming of chastisement if humanity's temptation to hubris is not ubiquitous and irresistible? The tragic figure exults in delusory inflation, suffers humiliation, and comes to wisdom through the restoration of the cosmic mystery of which he will never be the master. Tragic sobriety, sober wisdom. We moderns have scarce outgrown the need for such reminders.

The tragic sense of life, the tragic imagination of the human dilemma, remains most instructive to us. We know that the infant, and then the child, powerless to enact its own reality, at the mercy of the demands of the environment, both familial and cultural, "reads" the world as a series of messages about self and other and the transactions between. When the environment floods its boundaries, the child learns, irrevocably, its own powerlessness. In service to survival, the adaptive capacity of the child adopts attitudes and behaviors designed to promote survival and enhance the possibility of need gratification. Such a child may organize this provisional identity around the task of gaining power greater than that possessed by the environment, by avoiding its demands as much as possible, or, most commonly, seeking to give the environment what it wants in the expectation of reciprocity.

One cannot overemphasize the degree to which one's core psychology and behavioral patterns derive from this unavoidably flawed reading of the world and concomitant adoption of certain attitudes and strategies.

In the face of an insufficiently nurturant environment, the child will internalize this provisional message as a statement about its own worthiness to be met half-way. Identifying with this fantasy of diminishment, he or she will live out repeating patterns of self-devaluation, self-sabotage. Or the child will launch a frantic search for reassurance from the other, often choosing precisely those who will repeat the primordial experience of insufficiency. Such a desperate search for reassuring connection is the birth of addictions—through the connection with the other, there is a momentary lowering of the existential angst with which the child has always lived.

These readings of the world are phenomenological, experiential and essentially unconscious. They are progressively self-estranging. The greater the adaptation required, the more the individual suffers a split between the instinctual truth and the provisional, adaptive personality. This creates a spiritual alienation. As social adaptation is obligatory, some measure of self-alienation is universal. But the greater the adaptation, the more one suffers, for the psyche will symptomatically protest this continued wounding.[3]

In the face of this understanding of how we become strangers to ourselves, we see the relevance, wisdom, intuitive brilliance of the tragic vision. Fate presents each of us with a set of givens, a genetic inheritance, a family of origin carrying its own mythological burden in the unconscious, and a Zeitgeist loaded with implicit and explicit messages about one's identity.

None of these fated sources has anything necessarily to do with the

---

[3] [For fuller discussion of this etiology, and the insurgence of the psyche to promote healing, see Hollis, *The Middle Passage: From Misery to Meaning in Midlife.*—Ed.]

teleology of the soul, but they are powerful enough to entirely estrange a person from the soul's desire. We make our choices through *hamartia,* a wounded vision. The internalized phenomenology of childhood constitutes the lens through which one wanders in the labyrinth of choice. Hence the paradox of the tragic vision is our common condition; namely, we have made choices for which we are responsible, choices which have hurt ourselves and others, and yet we did not know we were making flawed choices at the time we made them. Who rises in the morning, looks in the mirror and says, "I think I will do something stupid today"?

Our hubris naturally manifests in the fantasy we all share, the thought that we know who we are, really, that we are able to consciously choose, and that we understand the dynamics beneath the issues which present themselves to us. Allied with our wounded Weltanschauung, puffed by our inflated fantasy of control, we choose our wounded ways, and then have the temerity to curse fate.

How humbling it was for the tragic heroes to find themselves to blame for the world of consequences, seldom because they intended malignity, but because they lacked sufficient consciousness, were not astute enough to know what they needed to know until life pounded them in the face and flung them bloody to earth. How humbled are we to find, in a thousand variations, that we have repeated our family's template, our old patterns in serial relationships, that we have embodied our unconscious tendencies in scene after scene. What the classical imagination expressed as the tragic vision remains profoundly true for us all, and helps explain why we suffer, and so often make a mess of our lives.

But the tragic vision flies in the face of the modernist dream. Fate is despised by Americans who believe that they are a new invention, that the old may be overthrown permanently and the world reinvented. In some ways this fantasy of self-invention is valid. A Swiss analyst told me once, "You crazy Americans. You get on a plane and fly around the world and get off and start to work. We Swiss would plan it all for years, figure all the possible negatives, and then not do it. That is why you are masters of the world." What at first seemed criticism was in fact admiration. On the other hand, Americans hate the idea of fate, the thought that forces of limitation, forces inherent in the structure of things, forces invisible to the sensate eye, are in charge. If we do not like this reality, we will move elsewhere and invent another. Such audacity does reinvent the world; and such hubris also careens toward a fall.

The chief fantasy of therapy, as we have seen, is the notion of progress through good will and insight. The general public believes three things of therapy and therapists. One, that therapists know secrets, and that, for a fee and a certain ritual, they will reveal them. Alas, generally speaking, therapists are ordinary people who know no secrets. One may more easily find the secret to losing weight, or finding romance, or improving self esteem, in almost any popular magazine. Therapists have little to offer on these fronts.

Secondly, it is expected that the therapist will be a good or bad parent to the patient. This is a more unconscious notion, to be sure, but it arises from the parent-child paradigm which is stirred by any supplicant coming before an empowered Other. We have all been there before and will play out the familiar relationships by over-identification with, hostility toward, or dependence upon, the parent surrogate evoked in the therapeutic relationship. As long as this transference remains unanalyzed, the patient stays stuck in all the developmental tasks which have brought him or her to the current impasse.

Thirdly, the public expects magic, that some shaman will venture into their psychic space, exorcise troublesome personal demons, and heal them instantaneously.

Were therapists required by "truth in advertising" legislation to tell their reality, then virtually no one would enter therapy. The therapist would be obliged to say at least three things in return to the suffering supplicant:

First, you will have to deal with this core issue the rest of your life, and at best you will manage to win a few skirmishes in your long uncivil war with yourself. Decades from now you will be fighting on these familiar fronts, though the terrain may have shifted so much that you may have difficulty recognizing the same old, same old.

Second, you will be obliged to disassemble the many forces you have gathered to defend against your wound. At this late date it is your defenses, not your wound, that cause the problem and arrest your journey.

But removing those defenses will oblige you to feel all the pain of that wound again.

And third, you will not be spared pain, vouchsafed wisdom or granted exemption from future suffering. In fact, genuine disclosure would require a therapist to reveal the shabby sham of managed care as a fraud, and make a much more modest claim for long-term depth therapy or analysis.

Yet, however modest that claim, it is, I believe, true. Therapy will not heal you, make your problems go away or make your life work out. It will, quite simply, make your life more interesting. You will come to more and more complex riddles wrapped within yourself and your relationships. This claim seems small potatoes to the anxious consumer world, but it is an immense gift, a stupendous contribution. Think of it: your own life might become more interesting to you!

Consciousness is the gift, and that is the best it gets.

2
The Core Complexes

As much as the term *complex,* coined by Jung, has entered the mainstream of modern parlance, its importance is generally overlooked.

A complex is an emotionally charged, internalized experience. As life brings us large experience, from pleasant to traumatic, so such experiences are internalized as partial mythologies, provisional identities, splinter personalities. As creatures of history, we are forever imposing that history on the present moment. The earliest experiences, our primal encounters with others, most notably mother and father, constitute what one may call core complexes, for they lie at the core of who we think we are, how we experience ourselves in the world, and what we expect of it.

A significant part of the dilemma of our lives arises from the extent to which we are owned by the core complexes. The world makes demands which the emerging personality "reads" phenomenologically and adapts to. This affect-laden adaptation constitutes a core complex which may become a provisional definition of the whole person whenever it is activated and subsumes consciousness. When consciousness is dominated by the materials of the unconscious, one is, for all practical purposes, in the past and not in the present. Moreover, one is thereby in service to a provisional, conditional construct which has the power to channel instinct, consciousness and identification away from the natural intentions of the Self, that central regulating force in the psyche.

D.H. Lawrence's *Sons and Lovers* speaks as eloquently as any clinical example. Even the title makes clear that before one becomes a lover, one has been someone's child. Here the core complexes show up autonomously to demonstrate the continuing impact of primal relational imagos.

Lawrence sets his novel in the Nottingham coal towns where he grew up. His father was a collier and his mother an oppressed and obsessive parent. Both turn up as the Morel parents. In thinly disguised fiction, Lawrence conducted a form of personal therapy upon himself, saying of his effort, "One sheds one's sickness in books—repeats and presents again one's emotions, to be master of them."[4] In the novel the father is sensuous, sometimes brutal, depressed by his burdensome life as a collier underground. The mother, Gertrude, says, "It does not seem as if I were taken into account."[5] Her understandable bitterness and depression is translated into despising her husband and projecting her unlived life onto her three sons, especially Paul, who is the *nom de plume* for Lawrence himself. While Lawrence later said he regretted making the father so pathetic and despicable, it becomes clear that the boy has no positive image of the masculine upon which to base his nascent manhood and by default must fall back on what a Jungian recognizes as the devouring animus of his mother.[6]

The imbalance in the marital relationship is experienced by the children and poisons them against their father, making them even more dependent upon their mother. "There was misery all over the house. The children breathed the air that was poisoned."[7] The mother rejects the father "and turns for love and life to her children. Henceforward, he was more or less a husk. And he acquiesced, as so many men do, yielding their place to their children."[8] The children pick up the message—their job is to please their mother by compensating for her unhappy life. How many children are likewise enlisted into the impossible, not to say unfair, project of making their parents feel good about themselves? When Paul gets a job, "his life story, like an Arabian nights, was told night after night to his Mother. It was almost as if it were her own life."[9]

As Paul tentatively begins his own entry into relationships, he finds himself strangely ambivalent toward the woman in his life. His mother is clear that any woman in her son's life is her rival and she does what she can to sabotage the relationship. Paul becomes conscious that when he is with his beloved, Miriam, he is somehow hurting his mother. As he is unaware that he is in the grip of a core complex, he begins to hate his

---

[4] Brenda Maddox, *D. H. Lawrence: The Story of a Marriage,* p. 151.
[5] *Sons and Lovers,* p. 12.
[6] Maddox, *D.H. Lawrence,* p. 295.
[7] *Sons and Lovers,* p. 45.
[8] Ibid., p. 50.
[9] Ibid., p. 134.

partner for seemingly triangulating him, little surmising that he is only playing out the legacy of his mother's fascination with him.

And when he wins a prize for his art, his mother concludes, "Paul was going to distinguish himself. Life for her was rich with promise. She was to see herself fulfilled. Not for nothing had been her struggle."[10]

In *Under Saturn's Shadow,* I cited *The Hand That Rocks the Cradle,* by Mercedes and Anne Maloney, as a study which demonstrates how profoundly a son can carry this message. The lives of many so-called successful men are dedicated to bringing home the laurels, if not for mother, then for the mother complex. In particular, a great preponderance of American presidents were "mother's sons," including Washington, Lincoln, Roosevelt, Nixon, Carter and Clinton.

Carrying this split imago of the female intimate other is common to all men, though it will vary from man to man. I recall one high-powered lawyer who spent much of his day running between his mother and his wife, each of whom had conflicting expectations of him. The power of the mother imago still carried by the personal mother and also, predictably, transferred to the spouse, kept him in the nightmarish situation of having to keep contradictory "mothers" happy.

In *Sons and Lovers,* Paul suffers this dilemma as well:

> Why was he torn so, almost bewildered, and unable to move? Why did his Mother sit at home and suffer? He knew she suffered badly. And why did he hate Miriam, and feel so cruel toward her, at the thought of his Mother?. . . Why did she make him feel as if he were uncertain of himself, insecure, an indefinite thing, as if he had not sufficient sheathing to prevent the night and space breaking into her?[11]

As outsiders we can easily see the power of the core complex which owns Paul, a power he senses but, as it is primarily unconscious, is transferred to Miriam. He believes he hates her, but it is the puissance of that primal imago which he hates, for it owns him—the more so as it is unconscious. That power transferred to Miriam compels him to resist her advances. "He wanted to give her passion and tenderness, and *he could*

---

[10] Ibid., p. 194.
[11] Ibid., p. 203.

not. He felt that she wanted the soul out of his body, and not him."[12]

It is natural for Paul to have this fear, for his mother complex has usurped his soul for now. As a putative adult, Paul is of course responsible for liberating himself from that complex, if he ever comes to know it exists. His mother is not a passive agent, however.

> "I've never—you know, Paul—I've never had a husband—not really." He strokes his mother's hair, and his mouth was on her throat. "And she exults so in taking you from me—she's not like ordinary girls." "Well, I don't love her." His mother kissed him with a long, fervent kiss. "My boy," she said, in a voice trembling with passionate love.[13]

In saying that she has never really had a husband, the mother not only seduces the eros of her child, at the same time she destroys his father and his potential for balancing energy. The cost of this intrapsychic triangulation is diabolic. It is not mother's love; it is mother's devouring neediness. I knew a man who stayed unmarried for over fifty years. When his increasingly senile mother was housed in his business office she would sometimes hold the doors shut tight. When asked what she was doing, she replied, "I am keeping the girls from my poor Joseph." She had been eminently successful at that task for half a century. The year after she died, Joseph married.

Paul Morel finds himself experiencing not only misplaced anger toward his beloved, but also fear. Such boys, as adults,

> could easier deny themselves than incur any reproach from a woman; for a woman was like their mother, and they were full of the sense of their mother. They preferred themselves to suffer the misery of celibacy, rather than risk the other person.[14]

Lawrence is stunningly candid about his own dilemma, and possibly that of how many boys who become priests or philosophers so that their eros can be put up into the sky rather than risk consummation, and consumption, here on earth, by the earthly. Lawrence had even asked his

---

[12] Ibid., p. 204.
[13] Ibid., p. 224.
[14] Ibid., p. 291.

mother's permission to engage the woman in his young life. Unwittingly, he tumbles to the power of the complex when Paul tells his mother, "I'll never meet the right woman while you still live."[15] (This all reminds me of a cartoon I saw once in which a Greek couple, sitting in lawn chairs, unroll a letter from their son. The father says, "It's from our son Oedipus. He says he's finally met a girl just like the girl that married dear old dad.")

When Paul's mother lies in her bed with terminal cancer, his deeply buried death wish is in part mixed with compassion as he mixes morphine with milk to give her, an oxymoronic inversion of the toxic mother's milk which he has inbibed. When his mother dies, he rushes to Miriam out of depression and dependency, but, fortunately, "she could not take him and relieve him of the responsibility of himself."[16] Confused, hurting, angry, Paul is finally flung out into the world. The novel ends with the implied beginning of his adulthood:

> His soul could not leave her [Mother], wherever she was. Now she was gone abroad into the night, and he was with her still. . . . He walked towards the faintly humming, glowing town, quickly.[17]

Jung has written about this necessary rupture from the power of the parental imago, but he sees the task as far more systemic than mere physical separation.

> The son tears himself loose from the mother, from the domestic hearth, to rise through battle to his destined heights. Always he imagines his worst enemy in front of him, yet he carries the enemy within himself—a deadly longing for the abyss, a longing to drown in his own source, to be sucked down into the realm of the Mothers. His life is a constant struggle against extinction. . . . The natural course of life demands that the young person should sacrifice his childhood and his childish dependence on the physical parents, lest he remain caught body and soul in the bonds of unconscious incest.[18]

---

[15] Ibid., p. 342.
[16] Ibid., p. 434.
[17] Ibid., p. 436.
[18] *Symbols of Transformation*, CW 5, par. 553. (CW refers throughout to *The Collected*

The incest of which Jung speaks is carried generically within each of us, the longing to replace the conflictual struggles of life with the satiety and security of returning to the womb, of remaining dependent upon the other. Who of us has not struggled, and does not continue to, with that archetypally regressive fantasy?

Clearly, Lawrence's capacity to bring his personal psychodynamics to the surface, to expose his own core complex, would seem to bode well for its transcendence. Yet, as we all know, Lawrence spent the rest of his life living out a strange ambivalence toward women. He worshiped them, feared them, idealized them, denigrated them. All of these emotions denied their individual humanity, seen as they were through the distorting lens of his archetyupal mother complex. He subsequently sought to privilege instinct over the mind, to exalt blood consciousness over intellect, in order to find some energy equal to the power of his core complex. The macho patina of his ideology was itself a compensation for powerlessness in the face of the feminine, as modeled by the mother. Despite his ability to articulate his core complex, we see that Lawrence spent the rest of his life in submission to its compelling power. The urgency of his writings was proportionate not only to the power of the complex but also to the summons of his individuation project to find and free himself.

What is urgent in our lives? What owns us? What do we seek to transcend? Recently I became aware of the power of a core complex, suggesting that old dogs still have much to learn. I found myself with strong negative affect after having visited a foundation in search of support for the institution of which I am the director. While I believe in the purposes of that institution, and can articulate its mission to anyone anywhere any time, I nonetheless felt discomfited by my visit. Coincidentally, that same day, in a weekly phone call with my father, I summarized the day's activities at his request. Humorously, he said, "You ended up a beggar after all."

The next morning I awoke with a recognition of the staying power of the core complexes. As we skirted the edges of poverty in my family of origin, we all adapted a counterphobic policy of pride. As children we

---

Works of C.G. Jung)

were not allowed to trick-or-treat at Halloween, ever, because it was "begging." Never mind that such play was harmless, and came out of a quite different value context; the proscription was expressive of the familial core complex. Nor was Santa Claus ever permitted because children should know whose hard work and sacrifice had brought them their gifts.

So going to a foundation decades later was a form, albeit many times removed, of begging. But that never held me as tightly as the counter-ideology of self-sufficiency did, and does. I found myself invested throughout my life in the fantasy of self-sufficiency and to this day fear dependency more than death or debility. How much that core complex, from which much seeming virtue may come, had owned me was the real discovery that awaited this old dog.

What is urgent in our lives? What owns us? What do we seek to transcend? These are the core complexes we serve and which govern our lives. They make the goal of creating a life very problematic indeed.

3
The Examined Life

In the summer of 1999 I taught a class at the C.G. Jung Educational Center in Houston titled "The Examined Life." Socrates, as we know, asserted that the unexamined life is not worth living. Why? Is it not easier to be a happy carrot? An unconscious ruminant?

Unfortunately, none of us has that option. That choice has been already removed by fate, and we are pitching on the high seas with no port behind and none in sight ahead. What Socrates suggests is that the examined life expands the range of vision and of possible choice. Like therapy, the examined life makes one's existence qualitatively more interesting. Indeed, therapy is the best way I know to examine one's life, which is why everyone deserves to have a significant therapeutic encounter at some point, not fueled by pathology, or problem-solving motives—though they, too, are often useful preludes to an encounter with the soul—but by the hope to make one's life more interesting. As Kierkegaard reminds us, "When a skipper sails a smack he usually knows his whole cruise beforehand; but a man-o-war only gets its orders at sea."[19]

Of the many writings by introspective figures one might choose, from Augustine to Virginia Woolf, I focus in this chapter on Blaise Pascal's *Pensées,* Henry David Thoreau's *Walden* and Søren Kierkegaard's *Journals,* because each is profound yet accessible. Each sought to know himself as deeply as possible through the exercise of a thorough-going personal analysis. As each was able to access dimensions of experience and analyze their personal meaning, and sometimes universal application, so they served and still serve others in their journey toward the examined life.

In a way, however, the examined life was easier for them than it is for us. We have less faith in rationalism. While rationalism for each of them

---

[19] *Papers and Journals: A Selection,* p. 371.

was a stay against tyrants and bigotry, we have also seen rationalism create monsters. We know much more about the unconscious. We know not only that it exists, is dynamic and always influential, but that inner space is as infinitely vast as outer space. Our more sensitive ancestors intuited this reality, as in Hamlet's observation that he could be bounded in a walnut shell and count himself a king of infinite space did he not have bad dreams.[20] But we know much more about the dynamics of the unconscious. We know of the power of projection, of repression, of sublimation, of transference, of identification, of autonomous complexes, of the shadow, and most of all the ego's Quisling readiness to be deceived, to believe what makes it comfortable to believe. We know that one can create an entire kingdom out of a complex and a world view out of an unconscious hunger.

Yes, it is much more difficult to be conscious today because we know so much more about the nature of the interferences and contaminations of consciousness. That is why therapy labors greatly to find extra-ego referents such as somatic symptoms, behavioral patterns and dreams which offer correctives to the blindness of ego.

In his imaginative rendering of Indian mythology, Roberto Calosso notes:

> What is peculiar about mind is that it doesn't know whether it exists or not. But it comes before everything else . . . even prior to establishing whether it existed or not, the mind desired. . . . A Self, *Atman*—that was the name it used. And the mind imagined that Self as having consistency.[21]

The brain is the organ, mind is the epiphenomenon, and consciousness is still further removed. We do not know what it is. We can no longer accept the Cartesian assertion that we know we are because we think, for we may suffer some delusion, some thought disorder, or some organic brain disturbance which confounds. I think I am thinking, but I may be wrong.

What Calosso calls the Self is consistent with Jung's view of the Self as that which is essentially mysterious, unknowable, but which expresses

---

[20] *Hamlet*, act 2, scene 2, line 263.
[21] *Ka*, p. 21.

itself autonomously and whose effects may occasionally be made conscious. The idea of the Self is simply a useful fiction (from Lat. *facere,* a thing made) that has no metaphysical reality. Moreover, it may no more be known by finite, limited consciousness than what is meant by the word God. But the Self is a useful fiction. It allows us to discern patterns, replication, consistency, which in time we differentiate through other words like character, temperament, even typology. What monitors the chemical processes of the body, what occasions dream dramaturgy, what expresses purpose through symptomatology, what manifests occasionally as consciousness, is apparently derived from an order of reality transcendent to comprehension, a supraordinant reality called the Self. It is, moreover, the apparent intentionality of this Self that accounts for our symbolic capacity and our potential for meaning.

Certainly Pascal, Thoreau, Kierkegaard and other inquiring humans intuited the presence of this energy we call the Self. Though, again, they could hardly have factored in what we are obliged to take into account— the role of the seething unconscious and the psychodynamic processes which render genuine consciousness more a hope than a reality. Thoreau expresses his intuitive encounter with the variegated psyche when he observes:

> I found in myself, and still find, an instinct toward a higher, or, as it is named, spiritual life, as do most men, and another toward a primitive rank and savage one, and I reverence them both. I love the wild not less than the good.[22]

He also intuited the presence of deeper, more earthy forces beneath the world of appearances, walking miles "through the deepest snow to keep an appointment with a beech tree, or a yellow birch, or an old acquaintance among the pines."[23] At the same time, the longest, most developed account in all of *Walden* is given over to the first chapter titled "Economy." Even in his agrarian, village environment, Thoreau perceived the enormous power of the emergent Zeitgeist to take one away

---

[22] *Walden: Or, Life in the Woods,* pp. 161f.
[23] Ibid., p. 204.

from harmony with nature and with Self. He saw how we can become owned by the things we own, humorously depicting a neighbor going up the street, metaphorically pushing a barn whose maintenance he was obliged to keep by daily servitude. He saw how humans become machines to sustain the machines they have invented to bring leisure into life, and how so many of us subsequently lead lives of quiet desperation.

He observed that we had steadily improved our homes but not the quality of those who live in them. He noted our enhanced communications systems when we have less and less to communicate. And our life is governed by fad, frenzy and fashion, so that what "the head monkey in France" wears will soon appear in local stores.

Meanwhile, Kierkegaard wrestles with the *gnothi seauton* of the Temple of Apollo at Delphi:

> One must first learn to know oneself before knowing anything else *(gnothi seauton)*. Only when the person has inwardly understood *himself*, and then sees the course forward from the path he has to take, does his life acquire repose and meaning. Only then is he free of that irksome, fateful travelling companion—that life's irony which appears in the sphere of knowledge and bids true knowledge begin with a not-knowing.[24]

Pascal takes on the problem of identity, knowing and being known, in the sixteenth century:

> And if someone loves me for my judgement or my memory, do they love me? *me*, myself? No, for I could lose those qualities without losing my self. Where then is this self, if it is neither in the body nor the soul? And how can one love the body or the soul except for the sake of such qualities, which are not what makes up the self, since they are perishable?[25]

While these explorers of themselves generally believed in a unitary Self, they also sensed its uneasy purchase on solidity. Such apprehension of the shaky solidity of things ripples as an angst-wave throughout Western history. One thinks of Hamlet fretting that this too, too solid flesh melts, and Prospero announcing we are such stuff as dreams are made

---

[24] *Papers and Journals,* p. 35.
[25] *Pensées,* pp. 217f.

on, while the phantasmagorical spectacle fades, leaving not a whit be-hind. In the East, the fatuous assertions of the ego are mocked by the death/rebirth cycle of Hinduism; and in Buddhism the Self is seen as an impediment to release from the cycle of suffering. It seeks the *Anatman,* which has transcended the world of desire and concomitant suffering. But what Jung meant by the Self is not so bound to the ego psychologies of modernism as some would suggest. Jung's views range across such artificial boundaries:

> The self *is* relatedness; the self doesn't exist without relationship. Only when the self mirrors itself in so many mirrors does it really exist—then it has roots. You can never come to your self by building a meditation hut on top of Mount Everest; you will only be visited by your own ghosts and that is not individuation: you are all alone with yourself and *the* self doesn't exist. . . . Not that you *are,* but that you *do* is the self. The self appears in your deeds, and deeds always mean relationship.[26]

As a matter of fact, while attesting to a supraordinate wisdom, about which many employ the homey metaphor of "the wisdom of nature," Jung asserts the multiplicity of selves, sees the Self as *doing* not being, and thus converts Self from noun into verb, *selving.*

The paradox of the Self as verb is beautifully and intuitively captured by the nineteenth-century poet Gerard Manley Hopkins:

> Each mortal thing does one thing and the same:
> Deals out that being indoors each one dwells;
> Selves—goes itself; myself it speaks and spells,
> Crying What I do is me: for that I came.[27]

The Self *selves*—for that we came, and individuation is the name. And yet the other side of the paradox is found in whatever guiding intelligence occasions that selving, which, in somatic, affective or intellective ways forever seeks its further expression.

In seeking that supraordinate wisdom, intuitively perceived, the West has depended most on mystics, authorities, scriptures, and reason. It is

---

[26] *Nietzsche's* Zarathustra: *Notes of the Seminar Given in 1934-1939,* p. 795.
[27] "As Kingfishers Catch Fire," in *A Hopkins Reader,* p. 67.

primarily with reason's staff that Pascal, Thoreau and Kierkegaard believe that they can pick their way through the bramble of uncertainty. For many moderns, however, the idea of a consistent, ordered and ordering Self is itself suspect. As Jungian analyst Paul Kugler puts it:

> Today it is the speaking Subject who declared God dead one hundred years ago whose very existence is now being called into question. No longer is the speaking subject unquestionably assumed to be the source of language and speech, existence and truth, autonomy and freedom, unity and wholeness, identity and individuality. The transcendence of Descartes' "cogito" is no longer so certain. The speaking subject appears to be not a referent beyond the first person pronoun, but, rather a fragmented entity produced by the act of speaking. Each time the first person pronoun is uttered it projects a different entity, a different perspective and identity. It is positioned in a different location.[28]

Thus, the putative, fictive Self *selves*, enacts, though the mystery of what enacts the enactment remains, and disappears into mirrors which reflect mirrors which further reflect in infinite regression to eternity. One is reminded of the story of the chap who visits the guru to ask a question of existential urgency, namely, "What supports this world on which we wish to stand?" The guru replies, "It is the great sea turtle which supports the earth." "And what supports the great sea turtle?" the anxious modern inquires. "It is the great sky turtle." "And what supports the great sky turtle?" Whereupon the guru cuts him off with a bored wave of the hand, "Don't bother, it's turtles all the way down."

What is to be remembered here is not that we have to make our fictions conscious, but that we have to learn to live with and respect the mysteries anew, knowing that our fictions are fictions. Such courage before the abyss of possibility is the only way in which the mystery can be honored. There may be no Self, but the Self is a useful fiction which helps us find an Archimedean point, a stance outside that of the ego, from which to question all other points. Making fictions consciously is sanity and pragmatism; making fictions unconsciously, and being capti-

---

[28] Cited by Connie Zweig in Walter Truett Anderson, ed., *The Truth About the Truth,* pp. 149f.

vated by them, is madness. Such madness is common to literalism, scientism, fundamentalism and most ego psychologies.

Pascal, Thoreau and Kierkegaard believed still that truth was achievable. Even if today we have removed the capital letter from Truth, and speak only of personal truths, they were not necessarily wrong. When the distant shore is beyond the physical grasp, or the imaginative capacity, of the mariner, it does not mean that it is not there, exercising its summons to discovery. The fiction which carries one forward through turbulence and spindrift alike, will nonetheless prove a useful vessel.

4
People's Stories

I shall now try to look calmly at myself and begin to act inwardly, for only in this way will I be able as the child in its first consciously undertaken act refers to itself as "I," to call myself "I" in a profounder sense.

—Søren Kierkegaard, *Papers and Journals.*

The chief cause of human error is to be found in prejudices picked up in childhood.

—René Descartes, *Discourse on Method.*

There is an old Hebrew legend that Yahweh created humans because he loved stories. One surmises that we would have been the source of many stories in any case, for our psyche presents its truths in narrative forms. It may also be possible that Yahweh's or Allah's stories are being lived out through our lives, though we dream that we are their authors. Nonetheless, the story of history is the story of the individual, and not only in the sense in which Thomas Carlyle and Ralph Waldo Emerson asserted that history is the story of the individual writ large, or that what we call history is "the lie to which the victors agree," as Napoleon is alleged to have concluded.

Each of us lives out a story, a dynamic narrative whose only consistency is that we somehow show up in each of the scenes. While the plot line may be unknown to us, there is one. It is composed, of course, of genetic, familial and cultural antecedents which are present at the moment of birth. I am not suggesting any notion of past lives. There are those who sincerely believe in past lives; I remain unconvinced. The principle known as Occam's Razor still applies. The medieval philosopher William of Occam argued that when multiple explanations are possible, the one requiring the least embellishment is to be preferred. In short, there are many other ways of accounting for these unconscious determinants, whether biological, social or psychological, than the elaborate structure required of the past lives thesis.

The stories we live out are capable of alteration by fate, by the influence of others, and occasionally by conscious choice. The narrower the frame of consciousness, the greater the personal chronicle plays out as fate. As Jung has observed, what is denied inwardly, will come to us as Fate. As we can only be partially conscious at best, much of the fate we would deny or decry, we have unconsciously elected. This is why patterns occur so often in one's life, even though one is rationally obliged to admit that no one else made him or her choose that person, that path or that behavior.

We are reminded again of the wisdom of the classical imagination which intuited this paradox. The gods set things in motion, but the choices are ours. The sum of those choices, and their consequences which may ripple through generations to come, is the story of our life. As Kierkegaard notes in the passage that heads this chapter, a considered, serious and sustained encounter with one's inner life is required before one can even begin to speak of that "I" which the child so casually assumed. Finding one's story, the examination of how it has played out, and the recognition of possibly another story which seeks to emerge, is the task of therapy, or any pretense toward the examined life.

A forty-eight-year-old woman arrives in a state of depression. She feels hopeless and helpless. Her two children and her husband demand all of her energy and she has grown resentful and morose. She dreams that she is in labor but cannot deliver because of a large black mass which obstructs her. The large black mass is her depression, the *nigredo* expression of the *massa confusa,* as Jung described the presenting state in alchemical terms. That the psyche seeks new life but is blocked by the depression is obvious. This is her current story, but the real story is what lies within that black mass which has the power to block growth.

The paradox of this woman's depression is that it represents irrefutable evidence that the psyche is not pleased with her life, her choices. Her symptomatology is proportionate to the oppression she suffers. The depression is evidence of the dynamic character of the psyche which wishes life, and whose healing will come only when a person has been obliged to stop and ask why such a black mass has appeared.

Other schools of therapy would try to remove the black mass by medication, behavioral modification or cognitive reframing—all useful tools for sure. But none really honors the depression for its insistence that one's life be changed. In that *massa confusa* a powerful will to life may be found, though presently it is obscured and unavailable.

The real story, then, lies not in her feeling stuck in her domestic roles but what *in her* blocks the choices available. When one learns of her parents, both critical and emotionally unavailable, one finds the unnourished child who has no permission to be who she is, whose existence is conditional and dependent upon the approval of those around her, and whose will to pursue her own calling has been blunted. The current demands of the family, legitimate or not, are overpowering to a will which all her life has been thwarted, undermined and channeled into service to others.

The real story is what is occurring in the unconscious where time is timeless, where the internalized experiences of childhood reign, the more so as they remain unconscious. One can thus thank the depression as a gift from the psyche which wishes that the old wounding be healed. New life is already in the birth canal. The birth is blocked by the black mass in whose core lie the contemporary challenges of will, permission and courage to stand up to what was once over-powering and which still continues to be transferred to the contemporary objects of her life.

To thank the depression as an angel, a "messenger" of attention and healing, seems bizarre to contemporary culture which pathologizes such manifestations and seeks their rapid elimination. The story to which her life is summoned, however, can only be resumed when she enters that black mass and recovers the capacities with which we are provided by nature when we are launched on this strange journey of life. All of the forces of her childhood sought to perpetuate her diminishment. The summons of the journey to embody one's story in the world requires a recovery of the largeness which our incarnation intends.

Centuries before the advent of depth psychology, Blaise Pascal wondered about his fitness for relationship. His mother died when he was three and he was to grow into an adult who chastised his sister Gilberte for exchanging caresses with her children. He writes:

It is wrong that anyone should become attached to me even though they do so gladly and of their own accord. I should be misleading those in whom I have aroused such a desire, for I am no one's goal nor have I the means of satisfying anyone. . . . I am culpable if I make anyone love me.[29]

The outer story of Pascal manifests brilliance as a mathematician who virtually invented probability theory, a scientist who contributed to our understanding of air pressure and vacuum states, an inventor of a calculation machine and a brilliant apologist for his theology. His search for God, his love of number, his passion for the unfolding mystery of the natural world, all contributed to the building of civilization. His eros went into discovery, his desire into search, and his passion pursued elusive certainties. Where life was uncertain, number could be certain. Where fate was cruel and capricious, one could gain a measure of control through the rules of probability and a rational, ordered "knowledge" of God. His mother's early "abandonment" was his fate, and his compensatory mobilization of his supreme gifts becomes his story.

Another story emerges from those brief lines quoted above. What they tell is of an abandoned child who believes himself unworthy. The unconscious always functions logically albeit often erroneously. The child has interpreted early, primal loss as a phenomenological statement to him, namely, that the world is uncertain and he as he is insufficient to win and hold its love. This powerful reading, or misreading, of the fate which befell him, is extrapolated to the world—other times, places, persons. Such a child believes that he is unfit as an object of affection, and will prove dissatisfying to others. Therefore, he warns them away, probably with no little success.

And is there not also, in that last sentence, a plaintive cry, and a great personal denunciation? "I am culpable if I make anyone love me." Of what might he be culpable? Is he guilty of evincing their affection only to prove unworthy? Is it possible that he has concluded, as other orphaned children have through the power of magical thinking, that who he is was somehow responsible for his mother's departure? We know children will blame themselves for divorces, for death, for untoward events,

---

[29] *Pensées,* p. 117.

and fantasize that they must either be condemned to such culpability or seek to overcompensate by achievements elsewhere. Pascal did both. He attained brilliantly, and in his own eyes remained unworthy of being loved. His announcement is a virtual warning to others that they will be harmed by his inadequacy. For such a gifted mind as Pascal's, such a reading, or misreading, is ample testimony to the power of early, formative experience and its continuing transferential power to dominate the life story. Similarly, another fate would likely produce another life. As Freud once observed, the child who experiences the unconditional adulation of its mother will feel invincible.

One may see that the task of parenting is comprised of the early necessity of reassurance, and the softening of the existential blow of separation we call birth, and then the progressive abandonment of the child, in stages he or she can handle, in order to leave home at the appropriate time as a proto-adult. As this highly refined task is delivered unto ordinary humans, whose own experience of attachment/abandonment was wounded, one can scarcely expect the patterns not to be repeated. Often the pattern is generated by fate, as when Pascal lost his mother; and just as often the pattern is repeated through the unconscious paradigm of relationship between self and other which dominates our developmental process.

If one can identify unquestioned, reflexive tendencies of one's life, those for which rationalizations are immediately available, one might be able to work backward to the formative experiences of which they are the "logical" expression. Then one might be able to image alternative attitudes and behaviors as possibilities. The presence of symptoms throughout one's life is ample evidence that the psyche has registered its protest, its silent corrective gestures from the beginning. An honest evaluation of one's feeling state along those junctures, will confirm even more that the adaptive personality never did feel right. Again, relinquishing the adaptive responses and defenses will feel frightening, but will reward one with a supportive psyche in the end. Pascal might have found himself lovable if his great mind had been able to disentangle the acquired story from the natural desire of the gods. That he could not is the trap of rationalism, and the source of the fallacy that we can know ourselves without some dialogic, corrective relationship to the other.

The "other" may have been found through a relationship with a person whose love for him occasioned the possibility of another interpretation of self and world than that which fate had so far presented. Or the other might have been an interior dialogue with the psyche, which dreams provide, and which therapy today attempts, and he might have been pried out of the egocentric trap into which we all fall. The ego feels forever imperiled, and will fortify its ramparts with whatever loyal servants it can find. But servants loyal only to the ego will only strengthen the walls within which the ego is trapped. Just as Pascal could admit in another *pensée* that "the heart has reasons which Reason knows not,"[30] still his reason continued to serve the ego and its henchmen, and the larger story remained untold. We can say that his wound hurt him into his genius, just as Auden said that mad Ireland hurt Yeats into poetry, but we also know that child had other stories to write, in which his formidable powers would have also been available. We would have heard of Pascal either way, but in that other story, he might have achieved a greater enjoyment of his humanity.

Kierkegaard, the melancholy Dane, took his life motto from the poet-philosopher Goethe, "Half childish games, half God in my heart."[31] He held himself to be carrying the curse passed on to him by his father, and he may have been right.

Søren's father, Michael, had risen from impoverished shepherding to middle class, mercantile success. As a young man on a lonely Jutland heath, cold, afraid, bereft, he had cursed God. Later he seduced Søren's mother, dominated her and rendered her virtually irrelevant in the affairs of the household. When asked why he believed in God, Søren once replied that he believed because he knew that the gods hated him.

Michael's fiscal success did not protect his family from one disaster after another, including the deaths of mother and siblings, and incidences of undiagnosed mental illness. Søren, the last of seven children, believed that he was to expiate his father's blood curse through his own suffering

---

[30] Ibid., p. 127.
[31] *Papers and Journals,* frontispiece.

and early death. He became a radical critic of his age, of its institutions and all that the Father might embody, and he became an object of scorn. "Don't be a Søren," mothers of Copenhagen told their children. He laments, "Methinks I have written things that must move stones to tears, but my contemporaries are moved only to insults and envy."[32] All the time he is haunted by the curse of his father:

> How dreadful, the thought of that man who as a small boy tending sheep on a Jutland heath, in much suffering and exhausted, once stood up on a hill and cursed God!—and that man was unable to forget it when he was eighty-two years old.[33]

Elizabethan tragedy in Elsinor, and Greek tragedy in Copenhagen.

Kierkegaard intuits that he is carrying more than the curse of the gods. He carries, as Jung insists we all do, the unlived life, the unconscious story, of the parent. Using the word "liberal" here to mean free-thinker, Kierkegaard writes,

> The danger is not that the Father or educator is a liberal or a hypocrite. No, the danger is that he is a pious and God-fearing man, that the child is sincerely and profoundly convinced of this, but notices a deep disquiet in the Father's soul, as though not even being God-fearing and pious would bring peace to his soul. The danger lies exactly in the fact that, in this situation, the child is given the opportunity to conclude in effect that God is not infinite love after all.[34]

Feeling cursed by the curse upon this father, exposed on the one hand to a stern, demanding *imago Dei,* yet an imperious summons to radical religiosity on the other, and doomed to illness and early death, Kierkegaard, like Pascal, considers himself unlovable, unworthy and short-lived. He scandalously breaks off his engagement to Regina Olsen, an act which, given the mores of the time, brings great public obloquy upon him. No one knows his motives, but the best guess is that he cannot reveal his "pathological secret," namely, the familial curse, nor share his

---

[32] Ibid., p. 312.
[33] Ibid., p. 204.
[34] Ibid., p. 471.

wretched, short existence with her, nor expose her to that other curse of the family, which I suspect to be a systemic bipolar disorder.

> Inwardly torn asunder as I was, without any expectation of leading a happy earthly life . . . without hope of a happy and comfortable future . . . what wonder then that in desperate despair I grasped at nought but the intellectual side in man and clung fast to it, so that the thought of my own considerable powers of mind was my only consolation, ideas my one joy, and mankind indifferent to me.[35]

Kierkegaard did as we all do; he latched on to his talent, employed it as a defense against the cruelty of an implacable fate—a doom-bound and depressed family—and with every adaptation grew further and further from the child with all the world of possibility before him. The one-sided adaptation to environmental demands produces neurosis, Jung concluded, for such adaptation privileges parts of the personality at the expense of other parts. If we were to apply a tourniquet to one of our limbs, we would at first feel pain, and then nothing. But that disregarded limb would in time wreak its revenge and grow toxic to the system which neglected it. Such compensatory suffering is our common condition.

As one of the most pyschologically astute thinkers before the invention of depth psychology, Kierkegaard intuits how much his life is fueled, as all our lives are, by defenses against anxiety. Elsewhere I have defined the provisional personality, that is, the acquired as opposed to natural sense of self, as an assemblage of behaviors, attitudes toward self and other, and reflexive responses whose purpose is to manage the anxiety suffered by the child.[36] Such an assemblage is repeated, reticulated and reinforced, becoming the provisional vehicle of the soul, even as it is also the instrument of progressive estrangement from it.

Kierkegaard was led to wonder what his life would be like without this adaptive personality in place.

> Deep down in every person there dwells an anxiety that he become alone in the world, forgotten by God, overlooked among this huge household's

---

[35] Ibid., p. 40.
[36] See *The Middle Passage: From Misery to Meaning in Midlife*, pp. 10ff.

millions upon millions. One keeps this anxiety at bay by seeing many people around one who are bound to one as kin and friends. But the anxiety is there all the same. One dare hardly think what it would feel like if all this were taken away.[37]

And what would it feel like if one were to operate out of the natural core of one's being? We do so act, occasionally at least, when we are most spontaneous or wholly in that moment. When the Zen master strikes the nodding novice, he does so not as chastisement, but as a summons to return to this moment, this moment which is all there is. The past is past, and the future is never here. There is only this now, now. Yet, as we know, and T.S. Eliot strongly reminded us, it is not the pastness of the past which is significant, but the ubiquitous presence of the past.[38] The compensatory activity of the psyche, through moods, dreams, symptoms testifies to the relentless insistence of the psyche that it be honored. When Jung defined neurosis as a wounded god he meant to suggest that the symptomatology which we would so quickly suppress is a dynamic representation of the wounding of some deep part of one's soul.

It is the power of the acquired habits of reflexive response, the depth of the unconscious, the subtle capacity and vested interest of the ego to deceive itself, which make it so difficult to discern that one is living out a reactive rather than natural story. It is certainly true, as James Hillman has averred, that the soul has a code, which sometimes does prevail over all obstacles, but it is even more common that the code of the soul is overridden by the formative powers of history.[39] Hillman makes Henry Kissinger seem born to be Secretary of State, the natural expression of a youth who was unfrightened by his Hitler Youth peers in short pants. But was it not precisely this early terror that drove him to seek sovereignty over others, boasting that power was the only aphrodisiac? Maybe the young Henry was born to be a politician, but he was just as likely to have been born to be a beermaker, or an actor or a traveling salesman, even an

---

[37] *Papers and Journals,* p. 274.
[38] See "Tradition and Individual Talent," in Eliot, *Critical Theory Since Plato,* p. 78.
[39] *The Soul's Code: In Search of Character and Calling,* p. 177.

exceptional one. But we will never know. As Thoreau observed,

> We know not where we are. Beside, we are sound asleep nearly half our time. Yet we esteem ourselves wise, and have an established order on the surface. . . . [Even as] I am reminded of the greater Benefactor and Intelligence that stands over me the human insect.[40]

The "established order" of which Thoreau speaks is of course the acquired personality, informed and skilled as it may be by the natural instincts and talents. Could we ever imagine our story, not as the reflexive response to threat, but as seen by the greater Benefactor and Intelligence?

Such a transvalued story is what we glimpse when we attend to our dreams, do active imagination, and otherwise give therapeutic attention to soul, whereby the dialogue with one's own large unknown enlarges the world we have known. Rilke once mused that we could never see God, an infinite mystery extending far beyond the capacity of our finite limits, but we might be able to turn and see the world as God sees it.[41] That is what analytic psychology intends when it asks ego to submit to an honest exchange, what Jung called the *Auseinandersetzung* with the Self, the archetype of natural purposiveness in the organism.

From this dialogue emerges a larger story than can ever be achieved by the narrow frame of ego's world. This is why rationalism and modern ego-driven psychologies are ineffectual. Such approaches only serve to reinforce the story within which we hunker down, the safe bunker of acquired attitudes and utilitarian justifications. Such stories are not the stories for which we were intended.

---

[40] *Walden*, pp. 264f.
[41] See *Letters of Rainer Maria Rilke*, p. 172.

5
Necessary Fictions

My known self will never be more than a little clearing
in the forest. . . . Gods, strange gods, come forth . . . and
then go back. . . . I must have the courage to let them
come and go.
>   —D. H. Lawrence, *Sons and Lovers*

I am a stranger and afraid
In a world I never made.
>   —A. E. Houseman, "A Shropshire Lad."

The true is the name of whatever proves itself to be good in
the way of belief.
>   —William James, "A Pluralistic Universe."

It has been observed for over two centuries now that we live between myths. "Myth," as it is used here, refers to those affectively charged images (imagos) which serve to activate the psyche and to channel libido in service to some value.

We are never without myth, for we are never not in service to some charged image. Such imagos may come from our *Zeitgeist*, from our cultural mores, from our family of origin, or autogenously from our intrapsychic lives. As a matter of fact, what we call a "complex" contains in itself a partial mythology. It has a world view, an affective charge, a distorting lens, a commitment to the time and place in which it was born, and an attendant scenario which we enact unconsciously. When a person has a powerful reaction to another, positively or negatively, he or she is in thrall to a highly charged imago, perhaps parental, perhaps of a predator, perhaps of an object of desire. We are never without myth. The only question is: do the charged imagos to which our psyche is in service support the teleology of our own souls, or are they inimical?

When one serves an imago consonant with the desires of the soul, then one feels a sense of harmony and ready energy flow. When one serves an imago inimical to soul, then one suffers, consciously or unconsciously.

Unlike physical pain, which may be all too conscious, the pain of forced inauthenticity may remain unconscious; yet it engenders profound suffering which one may internalize as depression, externalize as violence, anaesthetize with substances, or somaticize as illness. According to one study, such suffering is experienced as

> damage to the integrity of the self, which is a psychological construct that represents a subjective sense of identity. . . . Suffering as threat or damage to the integrity of the self entails a disparity between what one expects of one's self and what one does or is. A serious disruption of the psychosocial trajectory of a human life . . . can cause such a disparity and thereby compel changes in the sense of self.[42]

Most of us have lived with such suffering since our earliest days and have become so acclimatized to its persistent hum beneath the surface of daily life that we would scarce know what to do if it were otherwise. As Kierkegaard wondered, what would we do without persistent anxiety?

The structural anthropologists have observed that it is far less important to discern how humans live through myths than to discern how myths live through humans. Such constructs, fictions as it were, give value to and determine our lives, the more so as they are unconscious. When Jung went through his mid-life crisis in the second decade of the last century, he asked himself what myth he was living. He found he did not know the answer, but the question itself occasioned a profound point of departure for an exploration which he conducted the rest of his life.

Such a question must be ours as well. What myth are we living? Are we living out our parents' unlived lives, compensating for their fears? Are we in thrall to the values of the herd, which may offend the soul but keeps one compliant company? Are we subject to those splinter mythologies, the complexes, which will direct the rest of our life on automatic pilot for so long as they remain unconscious and unchallenged? As

---

[42] Richard C. Chapman and Jonathan Gavrin, "Suffering: The Contribution of Persistent Pain," pp. 223ff.

they were for Jung, such questions are the necessary starting point for the project of the rest of our lives.

What I have called the middle passage arises from the collision of the provisional personality—that group of behaviors, attitudes toward self and other, and reflexive responses which the child is obliged to assemble to manage its relationship with an all powerful environment—with the insurgency of the natural, instinctual Self. Sometimes this insurgency is experienced in the field of intimate relationships, sometimes in an affective storm from below, sometimes in reaction to an outer crisis or loss. The *passage* is experienced as an enervation of the former way of seeing oneself or of one's functioning in the world. One may desperately seek to reemploy the stratagems of the past, but they seem ineffective or unsatisfying. The exhaustion of the old is the occasion for the advent of the new, though we are seldom pleased to suffer that death which is necessary for older values to be supplanted. In fact, one may wander, alone and afraid, for a very long time in the great In-Between before a new psychic image will arise to direct libido into the required developmental channel.

The primary task of therapy, and attendance on dreams, for example, is to discern what images will arise from the dynamic, spontaneous psyche. The more one can align the world of conscious choice with the indications of the unconscious, the more one will feel a sense of personal harmony, whether or not one's choices are supported by the collective environment. This capacity to choose from within, as it were, is the one thing the dependent child cannot do. He or she will have tried of course, but the power of the environment is our chief socializing lesson for good or for ill. Only the more resourceful and courageous adult can risk the disfavor of the environment to chose a different course, or, in Thoreau's phrase, to follow a different drummer. In the end, such a choice comes down to whether one will give assent or not to what one is summoned to do by the Self. That summons is our vocation, the calling to become oneself, part and parcel of individuation.

There is another way in which the natural maturation of the ego, and the strengthening of consciousness, can help. In the course of one's life one is exposed to models of possibility other than those of the family of origin and the milieu in which fate places one. One travels, one learns, one incorporates the experience of others through the assimilation of other cultures, other world views. Indeed, the chief value of the liberal arts is to liberate one from the shackles of narrowly conceived possibilities. A liberal arts education broadens the spectrum of images available, and the limitation of such imagery is the chief obstacle of a life well chosen. What one needs to learn of special skills are more properly postgraduate specialties. If the unexamined life is not worth living, the ever-broadened range of imaginal possibilities, which is the necessary constituent of genuine choice, is.

When Thoreau went to the woods he was not in retreat as such. He assiduously studied every tree, every leaf, every pond, knowing that it not only participated in its own genus and species, but that it also spoke an individual tongue. He learned to make friends of, and dialogue with, these "conversant" neighbors. He describes how rich it was to walk through the forest, or sit on his back porch, and take in the immense complexity of the world which lay before his probing eyes. Can we moderns, with our flowing distractions, even imagine such leisure, such attentiveness, such mindfulness?

In addition, by pulling away from the distractions of his rural Massachussetts' life, Thoreau opened himself to the intimations of his inner world. As the outer cacophony dimmed, the orchestral range of the psyche grew more palpable. Behind the old saying that the cure for loneliness is solitude, is the discovery that when one is alone one is not alone, but present to a goodly company, in a very rich dialogue with oneself. The chief pathology of our time is the capacity of the world to distract us from this conversation. If the world was too much for Wordsworth in 1802, and Thoreau needed to step out of Concord in the 1840's, what then of us, today?

But there is still a much larger task for consciousness: *What would you like to be, what kind of person, when you grow up?*

This is a question we frequently ask of children. We often forget to ask it of ourselves at midlife when we know something is played out, that something does not work for us. In the midst of this disorientation, we are nonetheless gifted by the experience that some things do work for us, and that there are intimations, hopes, dreams (doubtless tinged with the reality of adult life as compared to the heroic fantasies of youth), and longings which have played about the fringes of consciousness for a long time.

If we are to assume that this is our life and not someone else's; if this is the only one we know we get; if choices are possible, and matter, then when do we plan to grow up, to take final responsibility for our lives? Who does not, at the end, want to believe that one *mattered*, that one's life counted for something?

Tithonus of Greek myth was immortal, yet found life empty because no choice mattered. He could reverse a choice at will—a century here, a century there. He asks a blessing of the gods, that he be given mortality, so that choice could be decisive, so that life could matter. They so blessed him, and so are we blessed. Our mortality becomes the mother of choice. Our choices becomes the measure of the worth of our lives. We all are living out those saddest of lines in the English language, the conclusion of Milton's *Paradise Lost:*

> The world was all before them, where to choose
> Their placid nest . . . .
> They hand in hand with wandering steps and slow
> Through Eden took their solitary way.[43]

Out of Eden, the sleep of childhood, into the fallen world of choice and ineluctable consequences, comes the meaning of life. In the Edenic state, there is no humanity, only instinctual drives. After the fall into consciousness, adulthood and meaning are possible, but only because mortality makes choice matter.

So, what does one choose then, if one chooses to grow up? As Shelley said in praising the necessity of the imaginative renewal, habit is a great deadener.[44] So is fear, and so is lethargy, the twin gremlins which sit at the foot of our bed each morning, each wishing to nibble away resolution and desire. They are the enemy, as well as the fact that permission to be

---

[43] Book 12, lines 646-649.
[44] "A Defense of Poetry," in Hazard Adams, ed., *Critical Theory Since Plato,* p. 102.

who we are was so often conditionalized in childhood that most persons have to attain that existential freedom along the way on their own. Yet, as Schopenhauer argued in the last century, will is the life force seeking its own expression. Will is more than conscious intent, though consciousness can hinder or help. Will is expressed through the body, through desire, through dreams, and through the evanescent visions we may have throughout our life, the vision of the larger life.

Most often, the anxiety aroused by the summons to a larger life is more than we can bear. The larger life is the soul's agenda, not that of our parents or our culture, or even of our conscious will. The agenda of the soul will not be denied though it may be repressed. It will show up in depression, listlessness, ennui and fantasies. The deep intent of nature is to transform libido into ever higher forms. As Jung suggested, the traditional task of religious and mythic imagos was to channel energy into evolutionary development.[45] With the erosion of such numinous imagos, their energy has retreated into the unconscious and become pathology.

Interestingly enough, Thoreau discovered this principle of choice as well. And, moreover, he suggests that one may be well served to live out one's necessary fiction:

> I learned this, at least, by my experiment; that if one advances confidently in the direction of his dreams, and endeavors to live the life which he has imagined, he will meet with a success unimagined in common hours.[46]

To live the life one has *imagined*—that is, the life one is capable of imaging. For image is the carrier of the psychic energy. No image, no container for the energy. Such images may be acquired from others, which is the sole reason for the recognition of outer heroes. Such images can be engendered by the liberalizing of learning. Such images can be carried in the mythological systems of one's tribe. And such images may rise spontaneously from one's own unconscious. Thoreau alludes to "dreams," not as dreams, but as visionary images which one's psyche has presented and which seem to summon the response of consciousness.

---

[45] *Symbols of Transformation*, CW5, par. 553.
[46] *Walden*, p. 256.

It is the endeavor to live the life one has imaged which constitutes the sum and purpose of the whole second half of life. One may say, without ironic intention, that most of the first half of life is a gigantic, unavoidable mistake. Not a mistake of deliberate intention, but a set of intentions which are governed by the unconscious mythologems of the provisional personality. As one serves these mythologems, so one is obliged to digress further and further from the natural, instinctual teleology whose becoming is our life purpose. Only when one has hit enough of a wall does one begin to radically question the implicit premises of the acquired sense of self. The agenda of the second half of life, or whenever such radical summons finally becomes conscious, is to recover as much of the intent of the gods as possible by serving the soul's imago.

Nietzsche's aphoristic paradox, that we are the abyss and the tightrope across the abyss, alludes to this task.

> Man is a rope, tied between beast and overman—a rope over an abyss. A dangerous across, a dangerous -on-the-way, a dangerous looking-back, a dangerous shuddering and stopping.
>
>   What is great in man is that he is a bridge and not an end: what can be loved in man is that he is an *overture* and a *going under.*[47]

The abyss which threatens and intimidates is also our radical openness of possibility. To cross over we are obliged to spin out the tethering rope from the psyche's workshop, to extrude as the silk worm does, from its own being, and to walk on our own imaginal gossamer possibilities to the other side. This involves a going-under of the ego before a going-over.

Thoreau continues his advice:

> [One] will put some things behind, will pass an invisible boundary; new, universal, and more liberal laws will begin to establish themselves around and within him; or the old laws be expanded . . . and he will live with the license of a higher order of being. . . . If you have built castles in the air, your work need not be lost; that is where they should be. Now put the foundations under them.[48]

---

[47] "Thus Spake Zarathustra," in *The Portable Nietzsche,* pp. 126f.
[48] Ibid.

While it is true that Thoreau writes out of a higher nineteenth-century optimism about will and improvement, his suggestions are still valid. We are periodically obliged to set aside the old things, be liberated into the larger, and then engage in a higher, larger sense of purposeful task. The problem is not the castles, for most people left their "cloud-capped palaces" behind amid the detritus of daily life and disappointment. The task is to provide the specific pieces, step by step, which construct a foundation under that vision. It is at this point where will is irreplaceable. Will is focused intention, and, given enough effort, will in time wear away virtually all obstacles. Often, of course, it is not the castle as literal goal, but the understanding of the valences of that castle, the symbolic values, which are to be attained in its construction. One need not be a professional musician, for example, to be near, in, around music and have it enhance one's journey.

The summons of the soul is embodied in the image of the castle. Consciousness is tasked with the embodiment of that vision in the real world where we live and create our lives. And, as a final reminder of good New England folk wisdom, Thoreau adds, "Let everyone mind his own business, and endeavor to be what he was made."[49] That is as useful a definition of individuation as has ever been written, and a sure prescription for improving one's society by taking care of one's own business rather than adding it to the common woe. As a Sufi prophetess Rabi'a al-i'Adawiyya said, "My love of God leaves me no time to hate the Devil."[50]

It is again useful to recall that when we use the word "fiction," just as when we use the word "myth," we do not mean "untruth." Rather fiction comes from the Latin *facere*, "to make." So, a fiction is a thing made, a construct, an imago which carries energy. The point in calling it a fiction is to remind us that it is a construct, not a metaphysical entity. When Jung uses terms like animus, shadow, Self, he is not describing actual entities. They are metaphors of process; they are verbs. The Self *selves.*

A fiction is a construct which organizes energy. We have no choice but to be in service to a fiction, for we are always in service to conscious

---

[49] Ibid., p. 258.
[50] Llewellyn Vaughan-Lee, *Sufism: The Transformation of the Heart,* p. 8.

or unconscious constructs. Often they are the imprints of cultural values, but just as often they are the constructs we call complexes—energy systems containing affect, mythologems, locus in the past, and a conditional *Weltanschauung*. As an old Bob Dylan lyric has it, "Ya got ta serve somebody."

The question, then, is who, or what valorized system of assumptions—yours, someone else's or, more commonly, the introjects of fated, contingent experiences? To serve a construct which seems the product of one's life reflection, which finds feeling assent from within, which gives meaning and purpose to life, is to recover no small measure of personal freedom, dignity and autonomy. Because we can never know what is unconscious, we can never be certain that what we serve does not have hidden springs, with a panoply of ready rationalizations to justify anything. This is why Jungian analysts attend to the intimations the body brings, the ready availability of energy versus the coercion of it, the supportive dreams and other sources of confirmation which lie outside the ego's facile tendency to collusion and self-deception. Also, as the Bible suggests, by periodic examination of the fruits of our work we may come to know more fully what our proper work is.

The construct which we serve, the fiction lived, is what determines the degree to which we have recovered the power of choice rather than the replication of ingrained patterns. For all the pessimism expressed above in the initial chapter, the power of existential revolt is enormous. As Jean-Paul Sartre once observed, the French were never more free, potentially, than during the Nazi occupation.[51] Daily they had the choice to collaborate, to identify themselves as captives, or to remain free in act and spirit. They could put sand in gasoline tanks, slow down production vital to the occupier, and, most of all, feed freedom's inner fire under the nose of the captor. Paradoxically, where we may feel most frightened, or lacking in permission, the ground for greatest movement into meaning will often be found. When we serve this counterphobic strategy unconsciously, we are caught in overcompensation. When it is consciously enacted, then life gains largeness in the face of constriction. The slender

---

[51] *Existentialism and Humanism*, p. 226.

thread of possibility is extruded across the Nietzschean abyss which both terrifies and invites exploration.

The measure of our lives will derive from the limits of our fictions served. In the first half of life, we have little choice but to accede to the omnipotent demands of the environment, of culture and family experience. When the Self's insurgency has been suffered, the chance for redefinition and redirection of life opens. Once again, amazingly, Thoreau comments,

> When the play, it may be the tragedy, of life is over, the spectator goes his way. It was a kind of fiction, a work of the imagination only.[52]

What kind of play has our life been, in service to what, or to whom? Do we like what we see, if we look honestly, and whose fault is it then? If we do not like what we see, then we are obliged to construct a fiction more worthy of service. If we are stuck, and know we are stuck, and we always do, then is there not some deep imperative to get unstuck? And is not the assumption of this responsibility for finding the right fiction to serve what we mean by "becoming something when we grow up"?

---

[52] *Walden,* p. 104.

6
The Problem of Spiritual Authority

Quisque suos patimur manes.
"We make our destinies by our choice of gods."
—Virgil, *Aeneid.*

The historian of religion Mircea Eliade observed that the chief problem of the modern era was the disappearance of meaningful rites of passage. No doubt this loss is profound, and, among other things, occasioned the twentieth-century invention of what we call depth therapy, whose chief mission is to help one discern one's own death/rebirth passage more consciously. But another way of looking at this matter is to conclude that the chief dilemma of our time is the problem of spiritual authority. Namely:

—*by what truths (fictive constructs) do I live?*
—*by what truths do I understand who I am?*
—*how am I to use my energies during this brief transit I call my life?*
—*by what points of reference do I make my decisions?*

These questions play out for us every day, whether we attend them consciously or not. If not, then life is on automatic pilot and one may live an entire life reflexively rather than reflectively.

Certainly there has been a fracturing of the consensual reality over the last centuries, especially accelerated in the nineteenth in the shift from sacred institutions to secular surrogates such as the state and economics. The author George Eliot mused in a garden in Cambridge that three great ideas had animated humankind hitherto, namely "God," "Immortality," and "Duty."[53] How inconceivable the first two were to her critical mind, and yet how demanding the last.

In many ways the Victorian sensibility made a god of Duty, defined primarily as compliance with convention. The good life was moderate, sober, civic, respectful and ordered. It took the rebels of the *fin de siècle,*

---

[53] See Basil Willey, *Nineteenth Century Studies: Coleridge to Matthew Arnold,* p. 87.

Freud's "invention" of the unconscious, and the madness of history plunging into the abyss of a world war to overthrow these dutiful pieties. Similarly, mythological values were split off forever from metaphysics by Kant's critiques and by the rise of natural science. The art critic John Ruskin lamented that the clink of the geologists' hammers seemed to ring reproachfully at the end of every Biblical cadence.[54] Religion for most ceased to be a felt apprehension of the transcendent and became an ideological affiliation, which is why Nietzsche concluded that God was dead. God was no longer a felt experience. God had become an idea, an ideology, an institution, no longer the living, autonomous God of history. Today the seldom-challenged autonomy of empiricism and deconstructionism constitute ideologies become virtual institutions.

If myth is the invisible plane which supports the visible plane of life, what happens when the invisible plane is no longer phenomenologically experienced? Invariably, such severance of our grounding in transcendent reality occasions an existential angst. While it is true that some folks manage to get through life quite nicely as happy carrots, or Alpine cows well-belled and udderly productive, and some folks still feel connected to that which is larger than they through historically charged, institutionally sanctioned images, most people feel this whiff of angst and react to it in profound, often regressive ways.

There is a large section of the populace which suffers the problem of spiritual authority unconsciously and seeks to numb it by addiction or materialism. Pascal warned in the seventeenth century that the implicate motive of popular culture was the numbing of the soul's distress through *divertissement*, diversion.[55] How could Pascal, or anyone, have predicted a television set in virtually every room of every house, with MTV, the Home Shopping Network, or even the informed constancy of CNN, which allows one to numb out and live a stupefied, vicarious life?

A growing population has briefly suffered this angst and quickly adopted regressive postures to promote a closed system. These folks are part of the growing right-wing, authoritarian, militant (that is, frightened)

---

[54] Ibid.
[55] *Pensées*, p. 37.

movement which ranges from the militia and survivalist types, to those who seek to take over school boards and legislate morality, their morality mind you, to those who simply project their fear onto minorities. The rise of racism, anti-Semitism, homophobia and both domestic and international terrorism, even in the face of education and increased social mobility, bespeaks a splitting, a projection of the shadow problem of fear onto minorities. Now that the Communist conspiracy, the Red Menace, has been overthrown, who are we to hate, who, pray tell, is the enemy? As in Constantin Cavafy's poem, "Expecting the Barbarians," we stand alertly on our walls awaiting the enemy. When they do not come we are perplexed, dissatisfied, even more anxious.

> And now what shall become of us without any barbarians?
> Those people were a kind of solution.[56]

There is a third group of people, including many of those reading this book, who are strong enough to suffer the angst of modernism consciously, who try to hold to the necessary tension of opposites rather than tumble into fundamentalist pieties. As they are open to the developmental, to the dialectical, they are thus open to revelation, for the gods are most present when our dogmas and attitudes are not enclosing and containing them.

When we reflect on the nature of spiritual experience we recall that it is phenomenological in character, that is, experiential not conceptual. The energy of the gods, call it "spirit" for now, conflates an image and renders it numinous. Because such energy is of divinity, it is not beholden to human constraint or fixation, however much our ego desires the security of such reification. But, as the gods are the gods, they move when they will, and that spirit leaves the image it inhabited for a moment or a millennium. What is left behind is the husk of the image, minus the energy. Ego will cling, of course, to the trace of the divine, and hug the husk which was once numinous. The loss of that energy, however, occasions a profound angst which arises out of the dissociation of image and spirit. This angst has historically been "treated" by the contrivance of

---

[56] *The Complete Poems of Cavafy,* p. 19.

dogma to address the doubts of the mind, by ritual which seeks the original connection by repetition of what was once phenomenologically spontaneous, and cultic practices which bring some comfort in the association of like-mindedness with one's tribe. These artifacts of primal experience in time become institutions, and progressively more and more remote from the original encounter with the gods.

We all know this is true. If these institutional forms really connected people with the gods, we could see the difference. The urgency to consensus, the hysteria of conformism, the slippage into totalitarian thinking, is the surest measure of doubt, disbelief and dissimilation. The person in a living experience does not have to define it, think about it, defend it, proselytize. Those who do have to proselytize are furiously at work defending against their own doubt and their dissociation from the primal encounter with transcendent energy.

Accordingly, the test of the spiritually mature person is the same as that of the psychologically mature. Just as the level of individuation we have reached, that is, the degree of potential consciousness, is the chief variant in the quality of an interpersonal relationship, so our level of psychological maturity begets the theological tenor and texture to which one is drawn. We recall the hysteria in some quarters, (as opposed to a technical problem which was anticipated and solved), regarding the Y2K problem as the calendar turned over. In certain quarters survivalists anticipated institutional shut-down, social chaos, and much more. Even with something as banal as Y2K one can see the mechanism of projection, of unreflective psyches projecting fears.

The test of a psychologically mature person, and therefore spiritually mature, will be found in his or her capacity to handle what one might call the Triple A's: anxiety, ambiguity and ambivalence. While all of us suffer these onslaughts and react reflexively, the immature psyche especially suffers a tension and seeks to resolve it quickly by a shift right or left to a one-sided solution. The more mature psyche is able to sustain the tension of opposites and contain conflict longer, thereby allowing the developmental and revelatory potential of the issue to emerge. Anxiety rises in the face of uncertainty, open-endedness. Ambiguity confounds the ego's lust for security, to fix the world in a permanently knowable place. Ambivalence, the fact that the opposites are always present, visible or not, obliges one to deal with the capacity for dialogue with that other. This experience often obliges a confrontation with the shadow, where the values rejected by the ego are not unlike exiles plotting to return home surreptitiously.

How one handles the inescapable problem of the Triple A's implicitly raises the question of spiritual authority. Is one to project authority outward to a received package of values, the institutionalization of dogma, rite and cult, or is one willing to assume responsibility for tracking the spirit as it arises from new venues? For the former, authority externalized is personal responsibility avoided, and the potential for the Triple A's assuaged. For the latter, the capacity to stay open to the dynamism of life, to grant autonomy to the gods, to allow enlargement through revelation, is to open to a more respectful relationship with the mystery that moves through all events. If we could define it, control it, it would not be the mystery. This is why awe and submission before the transcendent are the chief religious values, and most difficult for the insecure.

But such openness is very difficult, for our ego anxiously wishes to fence in the boundaries of the soul and seek control. An example of the difficulty of staying open to the ambiguity which mystery demands may be seen in an interview with a denominational leader who has, with the help of his cohorts, purged the pulpits and many seminaries of its professors. Whoever takes a symbolic approach to scripture, for example, stirs unacceptable anxiety in this man. After having sought to justify his purging cause, he turns to the question of authority.

> If there is a God and that God loves man, he is going to reveal himself. If he is God, he can reveal himself accurately. If you can't rely on an accurate revelation from God, you have nothing you can rely on.[57]

This set of assertions is superficially seductive. But it essentially takes the line of the Big Guy argument. Hey, is God a Big Guy or not? Well, one's first thought is inclined to be, "Yup, God must really be a really Big Guy."

---

[57] *Houston Chronicle,* July 10, 1999.

And the Big Guy can do anything, right? Apart from all the assumptions denoted by the recurrent "if's," note how this man of alleged piety has no problem delimiting the Infinite. God who is God does not have to reveal anything, even to the leader of a big denomination. The nature of the divine may well be the *Deus absconditus* to which some theologians have testified. But it sure seems hard to argue that the Big Guy could not reveal himself accurately. Could we imagine the Big Guy as learning challenged, or inarticulate? But nothing is said here about our limited capacity to comprehend the Big Guy, how persons of intelligence and good faith have different experiences and different conclusions, or how such revelation may always lie beyond our powers to conceive.

So, sentence by slithery sentence, the pious believer builds his case for the Big Guy, ending with, essentially, "If he ain't the Big Guy, what can you rely on?" Later in the interview he says, "Either you believe the Bible from cover to cover, or you don't." That fact that this either/or fallacy would get one flunked in a freshman logic course does not seem to trouble this stalwart. Is one to completely ignore the character of metaphoric utterance, to conclude, for example, that when the Psalmist says the hills clapped hands with joy, that appendages actually grew from the slopes of Judea? Is one to ignore the weight of sober scholarship assembled over the last two centuries? What would it even mean to "believe" the Bible? That its many contradictions and ambiguities are just what the Big Guy ordered so as to confuse his followers?

What pretends to be logic is in fact the rationalized defense against anxiety. Reason can be used to justify any crime, and usually is. Reason can create self-referential systems which, because contained, not open, can only reproduce themselves. Ego is very clever in seeking its own reinforcement, and in service to the reduction of angst becomes a closed system which is forever justifying itself rather than changing itself.

Another example, far from the seminary wars, may suffice. I once had occasion to have a long discussion with academicians on the value of introducing the expressive arts into the classroom at a prestigious American university. The committee confused the expressive arts with the fine arts, and claimed that their superior faculty was already ahead of the game. I responded, "The problem with the academic world is that it privileges its own experience of consciousness to the exclusion of others, and always ends by being self-serving rather than furthering a serious pursuit of the mystery."

As a recovering academic, I am aware that nowhere, not even the Church, probably not even the Congress, the Knesset, the Politburo, is there a lower level of debate, more emotionally inflamed and complex-ridden, than on campuses. Intellect privileges intellect, and intellect constructs its self-serving models, which is why complexes are flying everywhere, the atmosphere is neurotic, and why youth often come to despise learning. In short, sometimes even the brightest do not know enough to know that they do not know enough. Under the tenor of the tone of our academic discussion hummed the omnipresent anxiety of authority and the reflexive regression to self-serving, security-seeking argument, that would have pleased our purger of seminaries.

But it is easy to criticize. We all operate this way. The most important if unspoken principle of psychological analysis may be: wherever rationalizations are found, there complexes are present. And the more obvious the corollary demands, the greater the defense and unaddressed anxiety. Who of us does not daily fumble the task of balancing the management of anxiety with a modicum of psychological integrity? If, as Paul Tillich, once argued, God is the God who appears from behind the God who has disappeared,[58] who can bear to sustain the tension of such ambiguity when one's entire world view is threatened?

Yet, therein lies the task. On a national level, we have low-grade politics which refuses to deal with nuance and ambiguity. We have polarized groups who cannot see that they are hating a part of themselves. We see even today the legally sanctioned "sign-police" in the Canadian province of Quebec, presumably expressing the will of the *vox populi,* who cannot tolerate diversity and arrest those who do not have their shop signs in French. Indeed, the spiritual and political landscape of our time is in the hands of those who are governed by anxiety, ambiguity and ambivalence. This is why they seek power in the first place and respond autocratically, dogmatically and with no little totalitarianism. Prayers in the classroom?

---

[58] *Theology of Culture,* p. 97.

Why sure. How about a prayer to the Sumerian goddess Inanna? Oh, you wanted yours? But mine goes back millennia. We know how such dialogue soon degenerates into hysteria. And hysterical rhetoric is precisely the uncertainty of authority as it defends itself against its own anxiety.

The flickering flame of consciousness may only be carried by those who can face their fears sufficiently to take on personal authority for their lives. Their psychologies, their theologies, their politics, will be open-ended, not closed, for they will be able to bear the tension of opposites. The recovery of spiritual authority in our time obliges resumption of personal access to the gods. We may know we are in their presence, that is, in the presence of transformative energies, when we experience resonance, depth and enlargement through encounter with the numinous.

The principle of resonance suggests that "like summons like." The modern is obliged to pick through the rubble of ancient civilizations, here or there finding a shard worth retaining. And how does one know which shards to carry forward in the infinite jigsaw puzzle of the soul? When something is *of* us, is *for* us, it sets off the tuning fork inside us. It resounds because it has always been there, archetypally. The resonance within us cannot be willed; it happens. No amount of willing will make it happen. But resonance is the surest guide to finding our own right path. It constitutes an inner guide amid the imposing images of the outer world and the constant traffic of the intrapsychic world. Resonance is the deep resounding of our truth, when we find it, or it finds us.

To hear it, one must be attentive, faithful, courageous enough to break from the power of the other cacophonous sounds and hear the resounding of our soul's intent. The temptation to live on the surface of life is clear enough. When we are pulled deeply into something, even love, it hurts and opens us up to great suffering. But the willingness to open to depth is the chief way in which dignity and purpose return to life. We cease being small when we stand in the presence of the large. The chief symptom of our culture is its banality. The chief antidote to banality is the willingness to accept the transformative suffering of depth.

The encounter with the numinous is available to those who have learned to listen for the resonance, who have surrendered the appeal of comfort to the summons of depth. The divine world speaks to us all the time—through other people, through our dreams, through sociopolitical events, through meditation, even through accident. Possibly the most humble, the most faithful confession ever uttered by a person in the twentieth century comes in a letter from Jung:

[God] is the name by which I designate all things which cross my wilful path violently and recklessly, all things which upset my subjective views, plans and intentions and change the course of my life for better or worse.[59]

Can we imagine a more radical faith than this which opens to revelation precisely in the overthrow of the ego? All that we align against the Triple A's of anxiety, ambiguity and ambivalence is here embraced as the possible entry of the divine. This is a profound statement of faith because it honors the autonomy of the gods, the transcendent energies of the cosmos, through staying open to the possibility of radical revelation in any event, any venue.

The citation from Virgil at the beginning of this chapter—"We make our destinies by our choice of gods"—paradoxically is demonstrated by the sometimes terrible choice we have to make between fear and anxiety. When we elect the fearful path, we regress, we infantilize, we oversimplify, we cut ourselves off from development and enlargement. When we embrace the anxiety attendant upon our condition, we open to the power of the divine. Ironically, the authority we seek is to be found only in relinquishing the fantasy of authority, to remember that we do not know enough. Through this humble openness the gods will most surely come. As Cavafy has intimated,

... the more we try, the more we will spoil,
we will complicate matters until we find ourselves
in utter confusion. And then we will stop.
It will be the hour for the gods to work.
The gods always come.[60]

---

[59] *Letters*, vol. 2, p. 525.
[60] "Intervention of the Gods," in *Complete Poems*, p. 209.

PART TWO

Attitudes and Practices
for the Second Half of Life

7

Amor Fati, the Love of One's Fate

The more we learn of genetics, of sociobiology, the more we see the implacable gods at work, those whom we have grouped under the rubric of *fate.* What is fate, and why would we impute the gods at work?

Fate is simply the word we have historically ascribed to whatever is given, unavoidably given. When a mathematician proposes, "Let x equal . . . ," there can be no argument, for x is defined. Etymologically our word fate derives from the Latin *fatum,* meaning "to speak," in the sense of something spoken or decreed by a god. That something has been spoken does not mean it is inevitable. One may have a tendency to depression, for example, and that genetic probability will surely be experienced in the course of one's life. But how that plays out is strung along a broad spectrum of chance and choice.

For the classical world there were three Fates, personified as deities. They were: Lachesis, who gives a specific lot to each person; Clotho, who reinforces or ratifies this lot; and the spinner Atropos, who creates the web of cause and effect within which one's life plays out. For the Greek imagination, the world arises from the interplay of the Fates (that we are mortal, for example); *Ananke,* or implacable, impersonal necessity (for example, that all things fall in time to earth); and *nous*, cognitive mind.

How one integrates the fated depression, or compensates for it, or succumbs to it, is very much in the hands of the individual, in that very elusive term, *character.* The word character derives from the Greek *kharakter* which means a marking instrument; thus it denotes something engraved into the substructure of personality. One may have a tendency toward addiction, for example, and yet, through the will exerted by character, walk another path. Sometimes, even character seems fated, though we like to imagine it is something we have attained along the way. Few of us would admit to bad character, though there are many choices we would gladly disown. Who, or what, within us made them?

Fate certainly determines, or so we believe, whose aircraft falls out of the sky, whose auto crosses into oncoming traffic, who contracts cancer. Was it fate that made Gautama the Buddha or Jesus the Christ or Mohammed the Prophet, or their character? Were the gods at work, or were these and other charismatic individuals the product of their own free choices? Were they, as conscious beings, happy with their choices, happy with their fate?

The brunt of Nikos Kazantzakis's *The Last Temptation of Christ* is the terrible tension in the young carpenter of Nazareth, the tension between his desire for a normal life and the internal voices that summon him to a different path. His crucifixion is less the physical suffering than the tension between ego desire and the demands of fate. So, too, the temptations faced by these prophetic figures seem to stem from the contest between ego desires and the pull of a deeper, darker fate, leading in time to a brilliant destiny.

According to Kazantzakis, the triumph of Jesus is not over death, as his followers believe, but his capacity to accept his fate, namely, to embrace the suffering he is called to live.

There is that other lonely prophet as envisioned by Albert Camus in *The Myth of Sisyphus.* We all know the disheartening story of Sisyphus, whose hubris is punished by forever having to push a boulder up a hill, only to see it roll down again. Surely the most hellish of punishments is unrelieved futility, which is not only the fate of Sisyphus, but may well express the human condition itself. Yet Camus adds a radical defiance, a *cri de coeur*, a hope. He imagines that at that moment when Sisyphus descends the hill once again, forever once again, he pauses and smiles before pushing that stone back up. In that smile, Camus fantasizes, is our existential revolt against fate. In that moment, rather than being doomed, fated, Sisyphus *chooses* to push the stone. In his choice he takes the autonomous power away from the gods; he reacquires his freedom, and his dignity.

You might say, "What's the difference, he still has to push the rock." But Camus is on to something more than revolt, a gesture which may remain forever futile in the face of fate. In that mysterious, inexplicable smile, Sisyphus says *yes* to his life, a condition he cannot chose, but an attitude which is entirely his. This *yes* is the achievement of *amor fati*, the love of one's fate.

But what does it mean to love one's fate? What if one hates one's fate? How can we love that over which we have no choice? And yet how does the parent love the child who arrives broken and deformed? Is *amor fati* only a rationalization, a ploy to relieve one of the burden of hopelessness? Or is it possible, as Camus suggests, that Sisyphus is truly free through his willing submission? Certainly the great religions have often taken this position. For instance, the word *Islam* means submission to the will of Allah. We are told to live in harmony with the Tao, or to integrate one's *chi* or *shi* or *ki* through massage, acupuncture or acupressure. Recall the Buddhist admonition to find the face we had before the world was made. And don't forget Dante's assertion: *"In la sua voluntade e nostra pace."*[61]

The folk saying popularized by the Rolling Stones that we seldom get what we want, but often get what we need, seems to strike at the heart of this mystery. There are few things over which we have choice in this life, at least the range of choice which the heroic ego of youth believes possible. In fact, one of the chief signs of the shift into the second half of life is the move from the magical ideas of childhood through the heroic, necessary self-delusion of youth and early adulthood, to the sober experience of limitation and regret in later life. Few of us arrive at the second half of life with clarity, conviction, satisfaction, because life too often led one along a tortuous path, away from the road envisioned.

I could never have envisioned what my second half of life has brought, nor could many reading this. I could not have conceived of my work as an analyst, writer, teacher and administrator. As disparate as these roles may seem, they have one thing in common—the requirement that I work as a mediator, a go-between, an interpreter. It is my vocation to work with complex material and simplify it, make it intelligible, translate it, communicate its values. Apparently, I was born into service of Hermes, the god of in-betweens, of hermeneutics, and knew it not. As Hamlet suggested, there is a destiny that shapes our ends, rough-hew

---

[61] "In Thy will lies our peace."

them how we will. All my little ego decisions exhausted various paths until I reached the one the gods intended. Whoddathunkit?

Many of us have experienced our lives as guided somehow by some invisible agency. Some may have a continuing dialogue with their Higher Power on this matter and overtly solicit the direction of their God. Others follow their dreams and search for clues. Others seem led willy-nilly along paths which constantly confound their planning, hopes and expectations, but in the end conclude they are where they were meant to be. I have been in all three situations at some point. Sadly, some people always seem out of place in their own lives, strangers in a strange play. They may spend their lives *kvetching*, blaming their parents or society or luck which is seemingly stacked against them. Who of these folks is best off? The apprehension of a force at work which has nothing whatsoever to do with the ego's intentions may be ascribed to bad luck or destiny, but either way such encounters are humbling. As Jung observed, "The experience of the self is always a defeat for the ego."[62]

Amor fati, the love of fate, is in the end a recognition that it is *here*, in *this place*, in *this time*, in *this arena* that we are called to live our lives. Surely meaning will be found not by the ego's triumphant conquest of fate, but by its interaction with, enlargement through, and sometimes defeat by, fate. To live our lives here, in this world, in this time, is richly pregnant with possibilities of meaning. Meaning is not something abstract, something sought, though I surely sought it in learning as a young person. It is an experiential byproduct of a life lived in the way it is supposed to be lived—as defined by forces transcendent to consciousness.

Such a life will seldom arise from the design of ego, for ego's gratification is evanescent at best. Meaning arises even out of the places of great suffering, because it is the epiphenomenon of *amor fati*. Loving one's fate, in the end, means living the life one is summoned to, not the life envisioned by the ego, by one's parents or by societal expectations. The love of one's fate is not fatalism, resignation, defeat or passivity. It is an heroic submission to the gods—not my will but Thine—which leads to the blessing of a life lived as it was meant to be lived. Perhaps

---

[62] *Mysterium Coniunctionis,* CW 14, par. 778.

Jesus wanted to marry Mary Magdalene, drive a spiffy chariot, live in a comfortable suburb. The godly powers had another idea.

One of the most profound of Jung's contributions to the field of psychology is the paradoxical concept of individuation. Even today the term is misunderstood as egotism or self-absorption. Rather, individuation has to do with becoming, as nearly as one can manage, the being that was set in motion by the gods. Such a path is seldom if ever the path of ego gratification, creature comforts, vacillation and flight. It is the cruciform path of the Self which will seek its own fullest being whether the ego cooperates or not.

Just as Dietrich Bonhoeffer surely prayed for his release from Flensburg K-Z Lager, so he also prayed that in that mad place he might know God's will for him. He had been brought there because of his opposition to Hitler; it was not God who put him there. But his task, while there, before he was hanged, was to find and serve his fate with as much fidelity as he could manage. That is the model of individuation. It is not the path of solipsism, isolation, self-aggrandizement. It is the path of defeat which may lead to a life well lived.

Whatever one's fate may have in store, the task, if we are up to it, is to serve the individuation imperative, to become as nearly like ourselves as we can manage. *Amor fati* is, after all, even amid defeat and confusion, a form of love. To love one's fate is to embrace the loathsome frog, kiss the suppurating wound, accept the ignominy of defeat, and yet find that somehow one has been blessed.

Even Oedipus, whose crimes were so loathsome to his contemporaries that they exiled him for life rather than impose the lesser punishment of execution, suffers his individuation journey for twenty years and comes to the apotheosis of Colonus. Knowing that all was in ruin, he could still bless his life, for he had been called to know himself more fully than anyone before him. By serving this summons he blesses his painful world and is blessed in return.

The love of one's fate is, finally, the affirmation that the gods are the gods, and that our task is to find their will, wheresoever that road will take us. To take such a road, with even a fraction of the fidelity of Oedipus, will lead one to abundance. It is a not a fatuous optimism or piety that leads William Butler Yeats, hurting mightily in bone and soul in 1929, to conclude:

> I am content to follow to its source
> Every event in action or in thought;
> Measure the lot; forgive myself the lot!
> When such as I cast out remorse
> So great a sweetness flows into the breast
> We must laugh and we must sing,
> We are blest by everything,
> Everything we look upon is blest.[63]

---

[63] "A Dialogue of Self and Soul," in *Selected Poems and Two Plays,* p. 125.

8
Redeeming Ancestors

We read in the Bible that the sins of the parents are visited upon the children unto the third generation. This awesome truth is well known to therapists, who often compose an actual or a figurative genealogical chart for their patients, for they perceive that much of what is surfacing in the life of this person are the ghosts of the past. Those ghosts are inherited influences or psychic effects, some conscious as a result of exemplification, some unconscious as a result of the silent transmission of attitudes and behaviors. No influences are more pervasive, or determinative, than those of which one is unaware. We inherit not only the Zeitgeist of our fated time and place, but also the implicit world-view of the tribe and the family of origin.

As we have already seen, this silent, invisible cause-and-effect transmission was especially noted and brilliantly dramatized in the tragic dramas of ancient Greece, which functioned as a therapy of private and public psychopathology. Aristotle concluded that such public enactment led not only to a salubrious *katharsis,* but to the potential healing of the protagonist as well. Seeing the invisible cause/effect rippling through the generations, the tragedians mythopoetically construed the pathologized origins as some ancient curse of the gods for some ancient transgression of the elders. As a result of this transgression, a curse is placed upon a house, and its effects emerge in generation after generation until someone, through suffering, comes to consciousness and breaks the invisible chain. Until then, the whole lineage sees the world through this wounded vision, which the Greeks called *hamartia.* With *anagnorisis,* or recognition, the protagonist sees the world of choice from a wider frame of reference and then can finally make new choices.

Such is the voyage of consciousness, which we have all learned the hard way, with much more learning ahead, and such is the course of therapy which represents a somewhat more focused effort to analyze cause and effect in the contemporary individual. It is not that the focus of

71

therapy is on the past, as some believe; it is intensely on the present, which is infiltrated, contaminated, by the past. Jung's use of the word "contamination" is explicit. We fall under the influence of a complex, a psychological "idea," and as a result of that idea we make bad choices.

When Jung suggests that the greatest burden the child must bear is the unlived life of the parents, he is suggesting that wherever a parent was stuck in his or her individuation becomes an internalized paradigm for the child. That child *cum* adult either replicates the pattern, overcompensates for it, or seeks to heal it in outer life. In his talks to educators, Jung asserts that what educators teach is *themselves* rather than their subject matter, that students will take seriously what is professed by their teachers and disregard what feels inauthentic.[64] Thus therapy, whether formally conducted or intuitively grasped along the way, is forever the healing of history as it operates autonomously in us.

What we are seeking to do in our lives, then, is to redeem history, redeem our ancestors, for the work we do not accomplish in our generation will become the chief burden of our children, students, clients and friends.

But what does it mean to redeem our ancestors? I would suggest that we look at this notion in four ways. Of the first two I am confident, and the fourth I offer only as an intriguing idea.

1) *Redemption of ancestors through corrective action*

As suggested above, we either replicate our parents, especially as those matrices are unconscious, or overcompensate for them, or seek to heal them. We replicate our parents choices, and their level of individuation, by repeating patterns. Even when we know something of those patterns and seek to avoid them, we may find years later that we have repeated them. This phenomenon is especially evident in the arena of intimate relationships, perhaps because nowhere are the primal imagos of self and other more clearly evoked than when we are in an intimate relationship. The evocation of that primal imago is unavoidable, and often

---

[64] "The Development of Personality," *The Development of Personality,* CW 17, pars. 284ff.

discouraging.[65] Only a concerted effort to sort out the specific nature of our personal programming can offer hope of change, of new choices.

2) *Redemption of the parent through overcompensation*

In many cases the child become adult spends his or her life overcompensating. Where the parent was blocked by fear, the child plunges into risk. Where the parent was impoverished, materially or spiritually, the child pursues abundance. Where the parent was lacking in development, the child becomes an expert. Wheresoever the child says, "I shall be anything but my parent," he or she is controlled by that parent still. Deputy Fuehrer Martin Bormann's son became a contemplative monk. What would his life choice have been had he not had a murderer for a father?

The quickest defense of the complex, the charged imago, is found in the rationalizations which defend it. How many callings in life, how many behaviors, are seeking to heal the past by compensating for it?

Often, before giving a public address, never easy for an introvert, I have evoked the voiceless parental and familial past and reminded myself that I was now speaking on behalf of those who had not been able to speak. This conscious evocation of a parental imago has often transferred the energy of the complex to the capacity to overthrow the natural apprehensions of introversion. Such tickling of the dragon is at least a conscious compensation, and, when consciously employed, can stir large energy in service to a goal.

3) *Redemption of the parent through healing efforts*

The child may seek to heal the parental imago, and implicitly the parent, by some conscious or unconscious act which addresses the wound. This generally unconscious motivation is present in the lives of most people who enter the so-called helping professions. Their conscious intent is to be of service to humankind, or they say they find the work interesting, but they are often extrapolating the wounds of the family of origin to those of humanity in general. Thus the archetype of the wounded healer is ubiquitous. It can both constitute one's vocational

---

[65] For more on the pervasive influence of the primary imagos, see Hollis, *The Eden Project: In Search of the Magical Other,* esp. pp. 55ff.

calling and at the same time be the chief source of stress and burn-out as the primal wounds are evoked over and over again, unceasingly pulling the caregiver back into the place of wounding to suffer it anew.

Seldom does the public comprehend that the caregiver may be suffering too, and suffering not only the wound of the patient but also his or her own wound. Only psychodynamically oriented training programs pay much attention to this countertransference phenomenon. Once in awhile, it is an act of great moment for the health of the caregiver to walk away from the work. At that moment, he or she is unhooking from the impossible task of healing the parent. It is no more possible for the adult to heal the parent than it was for the child.

4) *Retroactive healing of parents*

It is useful to think that the work we do on ourselves in this life will not only ripple into the next generations, for good or ill, but might just as well ripple backward in time. Such an idea may seem preposterous. But we notice that the psyche has no particular interest in being constrained by the usual spatial and temporal boundaries of conscious life. The psyche can bring past and present together in dreams, through the invasion of complexes, and by embodying deep archetypal patterns in social life. Similarly, the psyche still operates prospectively, even when a person is facing a terminal condition, as indeed all our lives are from the beginning. The psyche does not seem convinced of endings, but images forth journeys, developments, enlargements.

Thus, it might be possible to fantasize that our work here might, just *might*, be healing to our parents, even those dead, and to other ancestors long gone. Possibly history is, as the critics speak of the Bible, the expression of *Heilsgeschichte,* redemptive or healing history. I have no evidence for this, but I would like to think that every injustice of the past might be corrected, that every frightened ancestral presence might find comfort and solace, that every stunted, deformed soul might continue to grow toward healing. I recall the occasion when I stood before the Swedish flag in a ceremony outside Stockholm and heard a "voice" which said, "I have come back for you." While I had no conscious intention of returning to the homeland of my Swedish ancestors, who had not themselves been able to return, I did have the unshakable conviction at that moment that I was carrying an ancestral task, and was in some small way healing an ancestral wound.

One need not posit theories of past lives, reincarnation or even a Heaven to have this thought—that possibly whatever was real persists in some fashion. Whatever was real, as psyche is real, abides and may continue to grow. Certainly our work involves the therapy of parental or ancestral complexes within ourselves. While we do not change past events, we do change their role, the effects of their programs in our lives, and how history plays out ever anew. Possibly this prospective work also works backward on these psychic realities and reformulates them. For sure the work we do today affects the future. If the history of the world is in some fashion the growth of consciousness, possibly the healing we attain personally will heal history as well.

9
Crisis

Which is harder: to be executed, or to suffer that prolonged
agony which consists of being trampled to death by geese?
—Søren Kierkegaard, *Papers and Journals.*

In the course of our journey we will come to many crises, or they will
come to us. Most often these events are unwelcome and intrusive guests.
Some are terrible and traumatic; some are time-bound and later even
seem trivial; all of them constitute the richness of a life which is so sur-
feited with experiences, including suffering or grief, that we can hardly
bear it. The Chinese ideogram for crisis consists of two pictures—one
suggesting danger, the other opportunity. I once received it from a stock
broker who, in a declining market, suggested I see the occasion as a
"dangerous opportunity" and send him more money. He could very well
have been right, though I recall seeing more danger than opportunity.

Possibly a more useful metaphor emerges from the etymology of the
word crisis, which interestingly enough shares the same root as the words
criticism, critique, critical and criterion, from the Greek *krinein*, "to sift."
Thus, *kritikos* is "able to discern" and criterion is "a standard or means of
judgment." Accordingly, the invitation of a crisis then is to sift through,
to discern what is important, to find what developmental task may be
required.

Jung has observed that crises come at critical points in our life. Usually they make it painfully evident that the previous world-view or attitudes of consciousness are inadequate to encompass the new situation.
Accordingly, the crisis requires the development of new attitudes, however disdainful the ego may be. Often these crises are tied to the exhaustion of the dominant attitudes of consciousness and are indications that
neglected portions of the psyche need to be brought into play. In fairy
tales, for example, one finds the motif of a king or queen whose land is
moribund, or under threat from some sinister force. Invariably, the re-

demption of the situation comes from the "little people," the dwarfs, the Dummling, the rejected soldier, the trickster, the marginalized child, for these functions, or energies, have a compensatory value for the kingdom. Such stories may be seen as the portrait of a neurosis, a one-sidedness that activates the transcendent energies of the Self which, in the service of wholeness, work to bring about compensatory healing.

As these psychodynamic strategies function in fairy tales, so they are operative in the psyche. Any crisis brings the limitations of conscious life to the surface and reveals the need for enlargement. Perhaps there is no better example than that of Job who was a conventionally pious man, obeying the laws and collective mores by rote, but ignorant of the living, autonomous, transcendent God of his people. When his world was overthrown, his life a calamitous crisis, he was brought to a new relationship with this transcendent force, maker of the heavens and earth, maker of behemoth and leviathan. He moves from the received piety of his ears to the existential encounter of his eyes, from the assumption of a moral *quid pro quo* contract with the universe to a radicalized experience of the terrible Divine.

Such, in microcosm, is the meaning of crisis for us all—the invitation to sort and sift, to discern, to move to enlargement, to outgrow the sundry comforts of the old vision of self and world. We may not welcome crisis, but we have no choice other than to suffer it. And, indeed, we may well come to look upon it as a turning point, where our understanding grew, our psychology became enriched and differentiated, and our encounter with the unpredictable universe exploded into theretofore unimaginable new vision.[66]

---

[66] [For a book-length discourse on the positive side of the quicksands in which we have all floundered, see Hollis, *Swamplands of the Soul: New Life in Dismal Places.*—Ed.]

10
The Inescapable Condition

At a recent conference on "the dark side of personal and public life," jointly sponsored by the C.G. Jung Educational Center of Houston and the Honors College of the University of Houston, a colleague of mine presented a deeply moving account of the self-loathing which washed over her when she found herself paralyzed at her father's funeral. The undertaker (a rich metaphor for a businessman as psychopomp to Hades) had requested that she assist in finding pall-bearers. She couldn't move, and, on the spot, lacerated herself with recriminations. Even much, much later she was still the chief witness in the indictment against herself. All of us would wish to run to her aid and say, quite rightly, that such events are archetypal in character, touch on the core complexes at the very least, and quickly forgive her for what she cannot forgive in herself—her vulnerable humanity.

Most of us find ourselves the chief prosecuting attorney at our own trial. Was it not Kafka who said that he considered his life a summary court-martial in perpetual session? I have come to believe that a person worthy of being taken seriously by others, at least by the time of midlife, will have dutifully, and responsibly, gathered a list of shortcomings, repeated failures in the presence of grand challenges, and frequent sojourns in the savannas of selfishness and cowardice.

Like Coleridge's Ancient Mariner we travel always with the albatross of guilt, pettiness and complicity about our neck. In *The Fall,* Albert Camus identified "complicity" as our chief crime, whether complicity before vast social evils which thrive all about us, or very private complicity which thrives in our avoidances, our rationalizations, our tacit agreements.

We are all Quislings before the soul's agenda, or even the conscious ethical standards we profess. Or, like D.H. Lawrence in his autobiographical poem "Snake," we confess that before the largeness of life we have shrunk, before the invitation to dialogue we have dissembled, before the invitation to depth we have skittered away. With Paul Tillich, we confess to the crime of banality, of flight from depth, commitment and integrity. Who is not guilty of banality? Many of us live in a guilt-ghetto, and we don't like our internal neighbors very much.

To have a hope of surviving the second half of life, one will have to find a measure of self-forgiveness. Tillich's profound definition of "grace" was the capacity to accept oneself despite the fact that one is unacceptable. Grace may be easy to offer to others, but very difficult to give to ourselves. Yes, the world is full of those who slip away into rationalizations and avoid the summons to responsibility, but those reading this book are perhaps among the residents of that circle of the Inferno who know where the buck stops. So my friend who bemoans her failure to stand tall at her father's funeral, stands very tall indeed in terms of moral sensitivity. Her nature is redeemed by her rejection of redemption. We are all worthy, as unworthy as we are, and are redeemed by our capacity to feel unredeemable.

*

Flies are so mighty that they win battles, paralyze our mind, eat up our bodies.

—Blaise Pascal, *Pensées.*

If, as Pascal says, the human condition is comprised of "inconstancy, boredom, and anxiety,"[67] we find that little has changed since the seventeenth century. The anxiety part is clear enough, for our condition is at best perilous and uncertain. But boredom in the face of all those distractions, those *divertissements?* And how many more of them are there today than four centuries ago? But diversion from what? Diversion from the great abyss of being? As James Joyce suggests in "The Dead":

The world, I've come to think, is like the surface of a frozen lake. We walk along, we slip, we try to keep our balance and not to fall. One day there is a crack, and so we learn that underneath us is an unimaginable depth.[68]

---

[67] *Pensées,* p. 6.
[68] In *The Dubliners,* p. 286.

So that is what we seek diversion from—no wonder. The more frenetic the diversion the quicker the boredom because, as with any addiction, the escape is momentary, the diversion ineffective. If it were successful, we would never experience boredom or feel the *frisson* of angst.

We return, again and again, to the edge of the abyss, the cracking ice beneath our feet, poised over whatever it is we have most sought to avoid. What a mess, what a dilemma, what a *contretemps!* So boredom is endemic to a culture which seeks relief, release, escape. The more we seek diversion the greater the concomitant boredom. The daily awareness of death, of the great unknown, the inescapable dissolution of all that we have built, is a constant mockery of the ego's imperial fantasies. But such a contemplation, like the skull set on their writing desks by medieval monks, stuns one to awareness of that fate which slides beneath the surface, and one day rises like a primal shark toward our thrashing legs.

Again, the dread, which is the condition, is an invitation to enlarged consciousness and, with that, some possibility of meaning. This is the life we get, not another. This one is short, for real. It is precisely its finitude which brings choice home, makes some freedom possible and decisiveness necessary. What is one waiting for—retirement, a lottery win, an unmistakable sign—to start one's life? Whatever fear blocks one now, is it not a greater fear not to have been here, not to have mattered, not to have lived one's life? Mary Oliver puts it directly:

> When it's over, I want to say: all my life
> I was a bride married to amazement.
> I was the bridegroom, taking the world into my arms.
>
> When it's over, I don't want to wonder
> if I have made of my life something particular, and real.
> I don't want to find myself sighing and frightened,
> or full of argument.
>
> I don't want to end up simply having visited this world.[69]

So that is how it is, then; death is the creator of choice, of value, the omnipresent reminder that something may matter in the conduct of this

---

[69] "When Death Comes," in *New and Selected Poems*, pp. 10f.

day's life. Maybe this is what Wallace Stevens meant when he said that "death is the mother of beauty,"[70] for not-being is necessary for being to be. The over-againstness of death makes life, and choice, possible and necessary. To be stunned into stupor, to despair, to be consumed by the evanescence of life is to miss the reason why our life matters—precisely because it is so slight, so precious. Again, as Pascal reminds, the reed we are is so easily broken by the wind's onslaught,[71] but that reed is a sentient being which becomes a partner with the universe, a partner which that universe needs for consciousness, for witness, for beauty, and for the possibility of meaning. Our small part is no small part.

Amid that "inconstancy" which Pascal places in his triad, what is constant, what remains true? Fate does, for sure, also character, the ingrained dimensions of sensibility. And what Jung called the Self.

As noted earlier, the Self *selves*. The Self is simply a metaphor for the process of the progressive incarnation of that meaning which is inherent in being. Just as Goethe speculated that the *Urpflanze* (the essence of flower) loomed behind each particular bloom, so the Self participates in the order of being which seeks its own fullness. What keeps constancy is that transcendent order in each of us which produces corrective dreams, eloquent symptoms, inescapable somatic events, spectral visitations and the like. It is that order which the child intuits as itself, an inner harmonic which it knows is his or hers.

The Self is that which directs us, ineluctably, even in the face of immense contrary pressures, toward ourselves. We may live in bad faith with the Self, but something in us knows that, and registers its protest whether we pay attention or not. Something in us pulls us toward ourselves, quite apart from how the ego or the tribe would wish to arrange things. Pascal concludes, "Despite the sight of all the miseries which affect us and hold us by the throat we have an irrepressible instinct which bears us up."[72]

---

[70] "Sunday Morning," line 63, in Richard Ellmann and Robert O'Clair, *Modern Poems: An Introduction to Poetry*, p. 93

[71] *Pensées*, p. 47

[72] Ibid., p. 209.

Most of us, when we look back, can see the gestalt of the Self selving through those most deeply moving currents which we know to be ours. Thus this inconstant being has its constancy, a constancy which survives consciousness, memory, Alzheimer's, possibly even death. We who are inconstant are yet constant. As Gerard Manley Hopkins notes, this crushed carbon and oxygen we are, floating wraith-like through history, is "immortal diamond."[73]

*

How difficult it is to walk that razor's edge between the great pull of history within the currents of our blood, and the fantasies of future wherein all will be ruined or restored. Pascal observes:

> We never keep to the present. . . . The present is never our end. The past and the present are our means, the future alone our end. Thus we never actually live, but hope to live, and since we are always planning how to be happy, it is inevitable that we never be so.[74]

At times, life seems to be something happening outside of us. What can we ever conclude it means? Who would wish to conclude, as T.S. Eliot did, that our only monument might be concrete highways and a thousand lost golfballs, a life spent hurrying there so we can hurry back here, killing some time in the meantime?[75]

Though we are historic creatures, that is, creatures of what fate and flawed choices have provided, much of what we do is on automatic pilot, genetically, cognitively, reflexively programmed. We need a rap on the head from time to time to bring us into the present, to be here, not en route from somewhere to somewhere. In my case, a recent bout with a persistent pneumonia, with too many trips and schedules to attend, got my attention, allowed me to begin to reframe choices, to say "No" more often, and to reevaluate priorities. A good rap upside the head once in awhile. . . .

A popular saying has it that death is nature's way of telling us to slow

---

[73] "That Nature Is a Heraclitean Fire," in *A Hopkins Reader*, p. 81.
[74] *Pensées*, p. 13.
[75] "Chorus from the Rock," in *The Complete Poems and Plays of T.S. Eliot*, p. 103.

down. It would be better to hope for some other way to pull up, reflect and reorder our lives. As usual, the poet has said it best. In this case it is Rainer Maria Rilke:

> Be—and at the same time know the implication
> of non-being, the endless ground of your inner vibration,
> so you can fulfill it fully just this once.[76]

---

[76] "Sonnets to Orpheus," ii, 13, in Donald Prater, *A Ringing Glass: The Life of Rainer Maria Rilke,* frontispiece.

11
Mentors, Teachers, Gurus and Sages

In the archaic memory of personal psyche we are all children in an unknowable world, subject to implacable forces, terrified and dependent, immeasurably vulnerable. That matrix frequently leads one to seek mentors, teachers, sages, gurus. The younger one is, the more compelling is this need.

Certainly, one of the great absences of our time is suffered in the dearth of mentors for youth, someone to help them bridge from the known to the unknown world. How painfully we remember casting about for models, for clues as to how to behave. Often the nearest role model was another confused adolescent.

Adults too are missing initiated adults to whom they might turn. Most adults today are uninitiated, in that they have not experienced a death/rebirth, or found purchase in a larger vision vouchsafed by some wise elder who has been there and returned, compassionately, to share what is needed. Very little on the contemporary scene offers much hope for wise mentors.

Jung was very clear, over and over, that a therapist could not take a patient any farther than the therapist had traveled. What is not integrated in the therapist becomes a roadblock for both, contributing to mutual projections and sometimes even leading to the acting out of a *folie à deux*. What training analysis seeks to do is work on the psychological process of the individual, to be sure, but it also attends in a concerted fashion to the issues of projection as played out in transference and countertransference phenomena, that is, how complexes constellated in the psyche of the patient constellate complexes in the psyche of the analyst, and vice-versa.

While there are no assured safeguards against the pitfalls of projection, the efforts made in analytic training to mitigate its consequences is generally not even attempted in the training of most psychiatrists and other therapists. The critical role of supervision by the more experienced learner, the possibly more integrated training analyst, is not a guarantee, of course, but it is a profound and sincere recognition of the importance of mentoring.

The absence of initiated mentors and wise elders is tragic, for it leaves subsequent generations bereft of that learning which is necessary to travel the world. Apparently, the disappearance of mentors is not only a contemporary phenomenon, for Thoreau makes the same complaint:

> I have lived some thirty years on this planet, and I have yet to hear the first syllable of reliable or even earnest advice from my seniors. They have told me nothing, and probably cannot tell me anything to the purpose. Here is life, an experiment to a great extent untried by me, but it does not avail me that they have tried it. If I have any experience which I think valuable, I am sure to reflect that this my Mentors said nothing about.[77]

I recall as a child devouring biographies of famous people, hungering for the necessary knowledge of how to live in the world in a way which is bold, purposeful and meaningful. I am grateful for the many insights I gained from learning, but I do not recall many lessons passed on to me directly, person to person, which later proved helpful. Like most, I blundered into the world, and later, decades later, tried to make sense out of the rubble. For many of us, the first half of life is an inevitable mistake, given the power of shaping influences on the one hand, and the relative paucity of wisdom from caring elders on the other. My experience replicated Thoreau's disappointment. On the other hand, Thoreau found his way through the conduct of his own experiment, mistakes and all. So, too, we all stumble through the thicket of possible choices, and in time, if we are very lucky, may come upon our proper path.

In chapter 6 above, on the dilemma of the twin choices between inner or outer authority, we saw that great masses of humanity defer personal responsibility to a guru, an institution, a sacred text or a compelling ideology. No matter how well intended, they cannot in the end wholly address the individual character of the soul's journey. In fact, for most institutions, the very idea of an individual journey is threatening to its

---

[77] *Walden*, p. 7.

authority and control.

One might try this test on for size in examining the character of any particular institution: First, does it truly permit, even encourage, dissent? Second, is individual growth promoted? Of course, the legitimate sacrifice of personal interest, and mutual cooperation, are hallmarks of most organizations, but if they fail either of these tests, their members, employees or acolytes will suffer more than they will gain. Since the chief, often unconscious, goals of institutions are to preserve the institution as institution, rather than evolving beyond its founding vision to something else, and to take care of their own priesthood or executive corps, the care of the individual soul is usually lost in the shuffle.

The search for a guru is understandable, given the power of the parental imago in the life of the child. As this imago gets locked in, the putative dependency continues. Just as Thoreau looked for help from his potential mentors, and I devoured biographies, so one is forever seeking an external authority to show the way. Yet when we see the great masses of humanity controlled by superficial and often prejudicial logic, streams of unthinking congregants entering churches as big as small cities, and paranoid projections onto such abstractions as minorities, millennial calendars and individuals of some prominence, then we should suspect that something is amiss. What is missing is the discovery, which I believe critical for the worth, integrity and meaning of one's life, of the guru we all carry inside of us.

Freud saw human beings essentially as biological organisms seeking pleasure and avoiding pain. Surely we are that, but we are also so much more. There is a hungering energy in the organism, an energy historically identified as spirit, a desire for meaning which the ancients called soul, and a constant, internally corrective system carrying forth the project of spirit and soul, which Jung called the Self.

The Self *selves*. It expresses itself through affective invasions, through the constantly shifting evaluative process we call feeling, through intuitions, dreams, bodily symptoms and unconscious behavioral patterns. A sensitive reading of these clues makes one aware of the activity of the Self. Not to have discovered this autonomous reality, this self-correcting system, this mysterious carrier of the energy of the cosmos, is to have lived one's life virtually without self-knowledge. If we do not know of the Self, then we know next to nothing of ourselves. We will have lived as strangers to the deepest truth which courses within us. No matter how intelligent, how sensitive in relationships, how productive in the world, a person living without some ongoing contact with, and growing respect for, the Self has simply been a visitor in his or her own life.

By whatever name one calls it, the Self stands at the core of being. It has very little to do with what the ego or the tribe intends, rather it is the carrier of what the soul intends. Jung was on target when he wrote *Modern Man in Search of a Soul*, for most of us have not realized that the guru we seek is there for us all the time. (Jung's book came out in 1933, when masses of humanity were relinquishing personal responsibility in deference to the hysterical rantings of their Führer, carrier of their dissociated shadows). This inner guru will not make our life easy, free of suffering, nor win the plaudits of our tribe, but it will, if we bring ego into cooperative relationship with it, fill our lives with meaning, purpose and a general sense of the rightness of our course.

To be sure, we are all indebted to those who have been our great teachers. When it came time for me to retire from academia, and I was saying good-bye to my last seminar, I choked up. The emotions were not engendered because I was going to miss teaching; I had no plans to leave teaching, only academia, which I do not miss. Rather, what flashed before me at that moment was a parade of great teachers who had taught and inspired me, and the tears I felt were those of gratitude. We all need to recall the words of the great physicist Isaac Newton, who said that if we have stood tall it is because we stand on the shoulders of giants.

But the paradox remains that much of the time we have also learned as much from teachers of another kind, those who have opposed, oppressed or thwarted us. As a Tibetan proverb has it, "Bless those who curse and revile you, for they shall become your great teachers." We may not bless them at the time, but later, with the sober view of hindsight, we may admit that we have grown as much from their actions as from the benign figures of our childhood. Just as we learn by going where we have to go, we learn most from those who teach us what we need, rather than want, to know. No teacher surpasses that autonomous pedant, the unconscious, who continues to upset the applecart of consciousness and confound its hubris. No teacher is more humbling, more illuminating, than the patterns of our own history. And no teacher is more illuminating than the unconscious which pushes us into regions of experience where consciously we dared not go, or which we studiously avoided. And how often do we thank this relentless, sometimes ruthless pedagogue?

At the same time, the task of maturation is to achieve the condition of the sage. A sage is not a sage because she or he is older, more experienced, more intelligent or articulate. One can be an old fool just as easily as one was a young fool, and all of us were young fools. A sage is a person who has come to know what is true for him or her, one who has been refined by the fires of suffering and achieved a modicum of peace with what he or she knows, believes, lives. A sage is a person who has come to know one thing, and know it well, open still to growth, correction and change, and respectful of mystery, in whatever form it may appear.

One can only become a sage when one has had great teachers, even those who repeatedly upset the apple cart, and when one has learned to reject gurus who are inflated and self-serving. The great teachers are still found in nature, animals, children, and the enlargement which comes through being open to mystery.

Whoever claims the mantle of sage or guru is ensnared in the trap of delusion. Someone who makes no such claims but whose imagination is fired by something is indeed a great teacher.

12
The Necessary Mess of Things

What we call self-esteem is a relative matter. We are supposed to have high self-esteem, and if we do not we feel inadequate. Most of us look at others and admire not only their accomplishments but also their presumed higher position on the self-esteem ladder. Personally, I do not have high self-esteem, and I do not know a single person who does.

Perhaps this self-esteem business is overrated. A person with high self-esteem is often one with a narcissistic personality disorder whose whole persona is devoted to hiding from others his or her secret emptiness. Anyone with a modicum of consciousness and a mild dollop of integrity will be able to enumerate a very long list of screw-ups, shortcomings, betrayals, moments of cowardice and generalized incompetence. Anything less than a very long list suggests either an undeveloped awareness or an act of great self-deception.

So, accepting one's failings and limitations seems to constitute the most modest level of conscious endeavor. If one is busy pursuing what needs to be pursued, is interested in something worthy, and finding it all getting more and more interesting, then one has scant time to brood on the pseudo-issue of self-esteem. Boredom points to a bankruptcy of imagination. The excessive preoccupation with oneself, especially that luxury of low self-esteem, denotes a poverty of priority. Do we really think the gods give a fig about our puny deeds, or lack of them? Should we not rather follow what our nature summons us to follow, through all the dense thickets of life?

Kierkegaard, the melancholy Dane who vacillated between bold imaginative risk and profound despair, reminds us of the proper relationship between the puny ego and the task of being: "Being victorious doesn't mean that *I* triumph but that the idea triumphs through me, even if it also means I am sacrificed."[78]

---

[78] *Papers and Journals,* p. 206.

It is easier to have poor self-esteem than it is to accept that our life is to be lived anyhow, in spite of, with all that risk, ambiguity, and then death at the end. How much easier to live the gray, shadowless zone of Eliot's Prufrock, or Dostoyevsky's Underground Man, than to live without reference to whether we win or lose, have good or bad self-esteem, and still, bereft of certainty and confidence, accept responsibility for it in the end. Kierkegaard notes:

> Many arrive at life's result like schoolboys; they cheat their teacher by cribbing from the key in the math book, without having done the sum themselves.[79]

To have reached the correct sum by having "cribbed" is to have lived someone else's path, not one's own. Kierkegaard would likely agree that it would be far better to have our own eccentric answer, whatever it is, than someone else's, however much it may be applauded by the collective. Elsewhere he says, "The main point in respect of every existential problem is its meaning for me."[80]

Life is a generalized mess, compounded by all our contributions, our fears, retreats and meddling. And then we die. But, as we saw in chapter 5 on necessary fictions, such messes are almost always the progenitors of possibility. Meaning is not something found, or sought; it is something experienced along the way if one is fully flung into the matter.

In his autobiography Jung repeatedly recounts his dismay at what he found in his unconscious, yet each time he concluded that some deeper level of his own reality was opening further to him. While he did not include all his screw-ups in *Memories, Dreams, Reflections,* the book was never meant to be an autobiography in the conventional sense. It was, and remains so, an account of the spiritual journey of one of the great souls of our time.

Kierkegaard, whose theological and psychological insights continue to inspire modern thinkers, wrote this in his journal:

> I have just come back from a party where I was the life and soul. Witti-

---

[79] Ibid., p. 64.
[80] Ibid., 207.

cisms flowed from my lips. Everyone laughed and admired me—but I left, yes, that dash should be as long as the radii of the earth's orbit————————and wanted to shoot myself.[81]

All of us have to learn to live with a sense of failure, the discrepancy between our aspirations and our accomplishments, between our hopes and our capacities. Even Jung, who to my mind is still a *terra incognita* in his profundity, felt his life had been a failure. He confessed to a friend:

> I had to understand that I was unable to make people see what I am after. I am practically alone. There are a few who understand this and that, but almost nobody sees the whole. . . . I have failed in my foremost task: to open people's eyes to the fact that man has a soul and there is a buried treasure in the field and that our religion and philosophy are in a lamentable state.[82]

Our journey through the dreck and dross of our messes is an invitation to an enlargement of soul. What a terrible disservice conventional piety has performed in suggesting that the realm of the spirit is bloodless, above the earth, ethereal and perfect. It is rather in the realm of mud and blood, defeat and despair, that the soul's fiber is fashioned. The mess of life is our mess. Questions of self-esteem are a waste of time, a diversion we can ill afford. There is more mess of things to make ahead; some of them will be our great teachers, some will cause us to grow, and some will bring the fullness of failure to bear on the encounter with the mystery. Great meaning will often come from such dismal moments; they are our moments, our meaning, and we will be entitled to them because we will have paid dearly for them.

---

[81] Ibid., p. 50.
[82] Cited by Gerhard Adler, "Aspects of Jung's Personality," in *Psychological Perspectives,* vol. 6, no. 1 (Spring, 1975), p. 14.

13
The End of Ambition

Citizens of Athens, aren't you ashamed to care so much about making all the money you can and advancing your reputation and prestige, while for truth and wisdom and the improvement of your souls you have no thought or care?
—Socrates, *Crito.*

In the second half of life we are invited to leave ambition behind, as well as a preoccupation with self-esteem. Ambition is necessary in the first half of life. As an affectively charged image, which is to say a complex, ambition is necessary to activate and channel libido in the service of development. Such development is obliged if youth is to be weaned from the sleep of childhood, the yawning abyss of instinctual lethargy, and the inherent dependency of the child's condition.

Without ambition we would never leave the abode of parental protection and nourishment, never find that of which we might be capable. Of course everything that remains unconscious, undeveloped in youth, including nurturant needs, is projected onto the object of ambition. If the object of ambition is relationship, social status, wealth or power, whatever, the fantasy is that such attainment will provide confirmation of one's identity and fulfillment of one's needs. And sometimes, for awhile, achievements do satisfy these fantasies, but only for awhile. One of the signal events of what I have called the middle passage is the recognition that, having achieved one's goals, one still hungers for the inexpressible.

The experience involved in reaching for ever higher goals is necessary to strengthen the ego. One has to have been in the world, upon such fields of play as intimate relationship and career building, and have experienced both achievement and failure, exhilaration and disappointment, to attain an ego capable of reflecting upon itself. Whoever has not attained a self-reflecting ego is at the mercy of complexes and remains in childhood, however powerful in outer life. When one sees someone still obsessed with "success" in the second half of life, then one is encountering a non-reflective ego. The reflective ego broods on the futility of its path, the mortality which always frames our condition and the self-delusion that such hunger begets. Initially, self-reflection may occasion withdrawal and the regression of energy, which we know as depression, but these are precisely the psychological states that lead to wisdom.

Paradoxically, the greatest achievement of ambition will be to attain enough ego-reflectivity to be able to relinquish ambition. This paradox is analogous to the advice that one has to learn the rules and master the techniques, so as to transcend them in one's practice, whatever that might be. One must first have thoroughly learned the basics in order to rise to the realm of idiosyncratic process, which is where true creativity is found.

Then what, one may reasonably ask, is one to do in the second half of life? What does one serve if not ambition? Kierkegaard took on the professors and preachers of his time and suffered their calumny in return. He observes that "one way is to suffer, another to have become a professor of another's having suffered."[83] He notes the facility and finery of the priesthood and concludes:

> An adulterer, a robber, a thief caught in the act is not as far from Christianity as such a priest just when he is most bloated by his own eloquence in the pulpit, for the robber and the others do not think that what they do is Christianity.[84]

On the other hand, he imagines a cleric who mounts the pulpit and speaks to his astonished congregation:

> To preach Christianity in surroundings like these is not Christianity; be they ever so Christian, it is not Christianity; Christianity can be preached only by its being realized in the lives we live.[85]

Kierkegaard notes that Christ himself, their paradigm, was spat upon, crucified, reviled and not "smartly turned out" for services. It being far

---

[83] *Papers and Journals,* p. 614.
[84] Ibid., p. 543.
[85] Ibid., p. 369.

easier to worship a paradigm than imitate it in real life, one goes farther and farther from success, ambition and other collective values.

Kierkegaard's point certainly extends far beyond the fight he picked with the professors and clerics. One is called to live one's values in the world, quite apart from the likelihood of success, validation or self-aggrandizement. The embodiment of one's vocation, the calling to be a person of value in the world, is arguably the chief task of the second half of life. One is generally in service to the world and ego development in the first half, but to be in service to the soul in the second half is quite another matter. The usual needs, understandable in childhood, go generally unmet, and yet one experiences the meaning of suffering, engagement and the potential incarnation of one's values in the world.

Thinkers other than Kierkegaard arrived at this place. The unknown preacher Quoheleth, who articulates the Biblical book we call Ecclesiastes, acknowledges that all is "mist" (not "vanity," as the word *hebel* has been mistranslated). Achievement is futile, death ends all, and the corona of absurdity and vanity hovers about our heads. Yet, he concludes that what one is called to do should be done with vigor, not because one will be victorious in any ultimate sense, but because one experiences such investment as meaningful, as its own reward. Similarly, Albert Camus asserted that the world was meaningful precisely because it was absurd. If it was a package of meaning, it would be someone else's meaning, would lie outside of our personal experience. As the world is absurd, one creates a world of values by virtue of the choices one makes. Death closes all, notes Tennyson, yet some work of noble note may yet be done by those who wrestle with gods.[86]

Turning away from the delusion of ambition opens a free space wherein things may be done for the sake of doing them, where value is found by value created, where meaning is the byproduct of service to vocation, not service to ego.

While it takes a developed ego to be able to relinquish infantile needs, such an ego is further called to relinquish itself in service to the terrible beauty of this world. Beyond ambition lies the freedom of play, sacrifice

---

[86] "Ulysses," in Louis Untermeyer, ed., *A Concise Treasury of Great Poems,* p. 299.

and participation in the mystery. Kierkegaard said it well:

> Socrates could not prove the immortality of the soul; he simply said: This matter occupies me so much that I will order my life as though immortality were a fact—should there be none, *eh bien.* I still do not regret my choice; for this is the only thing that concerns me.[87]

---

[87] *Papers and Journals,* p. 503.

14
Being Small, Being Large

Every time I get on an airplane I am reminded of how small I am, how we hurtle through the air in a pressurized tube, how precarious, how unnatural it all still feels, even after a couple of million air miles. This reminder of our smallness, Pascal's imperiled "thinking reed," is necessary and useful, for it keeps things in perspective. This need to keep perspective is what drives us lemming-like to stand at the ocean's side, or to look upward at the mountains.

Such a sense of smallness came to me when I heard Joseph Campbell say that if one were still clinging to the old cosmology of the three-storied universe, with Heaven up there and Hell down there, and thought that Christ's ascension was literal, well then, if his body were hurtling skyward at the speed of light, 186,000 miles per second, his body would still be within our solar system, detectable by our current theodolite (interesting word, that) telemetry. Or think of the space which permeates even the solid appearance of the molecules of one's desk. A golf ball, floating in an area the size of Manhattan, would represent a single electron in a cavernous space. Such metaphors make one feel proportionately, and properly, small.

On the other hand, it is the pettiness of our lives which is so maddening. As Pascal noted, if Cleopatra's nose had been a quarter-inch longer, history would have unfolded differently.[88] We find our lives filled with the din of television shows devoted to voyeurism, trivial diversions, banality and pettiness. Why should one be preoccupied with fashion, with what is *au courant*, when one's real journey is mortal, mysterious and part of some larger agenda? Why should one waste one's energy in bigotry? Do I not have enough displaced parts of my own psyche to attend? Why should one be devoted to revenge, to vindication, to being right, when the great mysteries wheel all about us?

---

[88] *Pensées,* p. 120.

When I was a child and had no particular concept of divinity, and certainly no idea of molecular structure, I imagined that the world, which I knew to be a sphere, was one drop (molecule) in the dream of some cosmic dream, or thinker. And I knew that that thinker could, at a whim, have another thought, another dream, and all that I knew and was would vanish. It was a chilling notion and yet was irresistible and fascinating. It was not petty. Jung recalled lying on a rock thinking of the rock, and wondering if the rock was thinking him. These are not the idle daydreams of wastrel youth; they are efforts to conjure with the fundamental mystery of life.

We have all awakened from a moving dream, still in that space, still in the short corridor between worlds, and then resumed the identity of waking life. We privilege the identity of conscious life, but is it too not provisional an assumption? Could it be that privileging the conscious sense of self is an example of the Buddhist "monkey mind"—the nervous, self-preoccupied delusory mind? While the release of the fixation on the idea of a stable, knowable identity may feel vertiginous, it is not petty.

I am not suggesting that we spend our lives preoccupied with such thoughts, but our psychologies, our politics, our theologies, are trivial without them. While the conscious mind rejects such imaginal journeys, the unconscious mind not only embraces them but autonomously takes us to exotic places, places which may really be our home, rather than the petty places of television talk and game shows.

Surely the most dismal of epitaphs would read: "Here lies a petty person, one who took no imaginal journey, who died without ever having wandered or wondered."

15
Getting Over It . . .

How self-hood begins
with the walking away,
and love is proved
in the letting go.
— C. Day-Lewis, "Walking Away."

When we see a person still nursing a wound, years after the fact, still blaming another for their life, years after the fact, still embittered by injustice, years after the fact, we see not only someone who is stuck, but one who has never fully picked up responsibility for his or her life. Of course betrayal stings, injustice wounds, loss hurts, but the question remains—how much of oneself was invested, and how much energy so invested has never been brought back home? Similarly, those who set themselves up in judgment of others are either naive, inflated or unconsciously possessed by a super-ego system.

I confess to having umpired once, and after a close call that seemed to inflame everyone, I realized that if I was not prepared to be a Solomon, I was not prepared to be a pariah either, and quickly retired from the job. But later, I wondered what people expected from an umpire—that all the calls go their way? We grow inflamed if the referee does not favor our team, our child, our cause. We bridle at the thought that life is unfair, that bad judgments are sometimes the only ones possible, and that we and our cause will lose down the line in any case. No umpire, referee or prophet will be welcome with such news, ever.

The old French maxim, *tout comprend, tout pardoner* (to understand all is to forgive all) suggests that if we truly knew the roots of each person's experience, and if all behaviors flow "logically" from their springs, we would be able to forgive them. If this were true and generally accepted, we would have few if any prisons, no umpires, no death sentences—everyone would be safe at second. In our world of instant replay we rail against purblind umpires, but live with daily injustice, blind fate, capricious gods and only feeble protest. Since we cannot indict the gods, let us at least kill the umpire.

As a youth, and later in the first half of life, I was inflamed at the merest hint of injustice. I rallied for causes, and even went to theology school for awhile in order to build a case against God. In every course, I somehow managed to work the material around to the problem of theodicy, the gap between the imputation of an omniscient, omnipotent God of justice and compassion, and the obvious presence in the world of unredeemed suffering and injustice. I traveled to Dachau, Bergen-Belsen and Mauthausen with my children so that they would see where the bigotry train traveled. Even to this day, I can quickly grow incensed at the thought of the strong picking on the weak. But the old fire is mostly out.

I will never know why I was allowed to live a privileged life in a privileged country in a privileged century, and did not, as a child, ride one of those terrible trains to Treblinka. I know that people are still tortured and languish in fear and injustice everywhere, that ethnic cleansing still rears its hydra-head, that petty tin-horn dictators still cause great grief. I once found solace in an easy atheism, then an uneasy agnosticism, and today fall back on the oldest cliché of them all. I really do not have any idea what runs the universe, but I do know that compassion for others is the only thing which makes the bloody trip worth it.

As we have seen, ambition is a delusion, self-esteem a diversion. It all ends in dissolution in any case. Yet my life is full of meaning—in intellectual query, in aesthetic delight, in relationships, in good work—and I grow more capable of loving others through the injustice, blind stupidity and absurdity of it all.

It is a blooming mystery, as it always was, but I am more resigned than ever before to living with it as best I can, with attitudes and practices which make sense of my small part of it. This is not the certainty the youth sought, not the indictment of God which could never work since the Party of the First Part does not accept subpoenas from the Party of the Second Part. Nor is it any resolution. Yet, living with mystery, with ambiguity, anxiety and ambivalence, is to my mind still a better living.

16
Attending the Soul

The title of this chapter is the literal translation of the Greek word *psychotherapy*. While attitudes have changed since earlier in this century, it is astonishing to see that psychotherapy is still so misunderstood by the collective. No doubt some of this derives from the continuing false analogy of psychotherapy with the practice of medicine, the false analogy of spiritual suffering and biological disease, and the false analogy of cure and healing.

While much of the apprehension and judgmental attitude toward therapy is based on a fundamental fear of the nonrational world, and a general aversion to working with one's own unconscious, much of the blame must be laid at the door of modern practitioners of therapy, especially psychiatry. In seeking scientific verification of success, many of these practitioners have narrowed the definitions of pathology to behavioral patterns, faulty cognitions and flawed chemistry.

While it is certainly true that we are behaviors, and behaviors may be corrected, and we are cognitions which may be challenged by other cognitions, and we are chemical processes which may be compensated by other chemical processes, none of these modalities—behaviorism, cognitive restructuring and psychopharmacology—should be confused with psychotherapy. True, the best approach to such disorders as schizophrenia, bipolar disorder, obsessive-compulsive disorder, and endogenous depressions is medication. But what psychotherapy seeks to address is the whole person, the sum of behaviors, thoughts, chemical process and more—the meaning of that person, the meaning of his or her suffering and the meaning of his or her journey.

Psychotherapy, especially its analytic form, must reclaim its rooting in the life of the spirit, must insist that it is less of the world of empiricism than of the world once dominated by pastoral counseling. Analysts concerned to make themselves respectable to their colleagues in other schools of psychology and psychiatry lack the courage of their convictions. In seeking the approval of others, they risk vitiating the contribution that analytic psychology has brought, and continues to bring, to the world.

Most analytically-oriented therapists I know are comfortable with the stratagems of behavioral modification, and working with complexes certainly involves cognitive restructuring. They have no hesitation in referring analysands for medication on an as-needed basis. But they are able to distinguish between the frequently confused goals of cure and of healing. Cure arises from the disease model of medicine. We have a disease which we die of or triumph over. Healing has to do rather with the task of meaning. When Jung suggested that neurosis is suffering which has not yet found its meaning, he clearly did not rule out suffering. When the meaning of inner conflict is discerned, and the personal path of individuation becomes clearer, one may still suffer greatly, but one will also experience the meaning which flows from finding that personal path.

Healing, then, does not mean that one will reach an end-point where all is clear and conflict-free. Rather, we will go on from soul-wrenching conflict to soul-wrenching conflict, but we will also be growing through the process. Jung made this abundantly clear:

> There is a widespread prejudice that analysis is something like a "cure," to which one submits for a time and is then discharged healed. That is an . . . error left over from the early days of psychoanalysis. Analytical treatment could be described as a readjustment of a psychological attitude. . . . [but] there is no change that is unconditionally valid over a long period of time.[89]

The "psychological attitude" of which Jung speaks is invariably influenced by a domineering complex, the internalized mythology of another time and place, which blinds one to environmental changes and the soul's deeper intention. How could we imagine that the attitudes of one stage of our life would be adequate for subsequent stages and altered realities? While it is the secret hope of the nervous ego to fix the world and render it more predictable and secure, all is in flux; what worked yesterday has become today's obstruction. Finding the secret sources of our

---

[89] "The Transcendent Function," *The Structure and Dynamics of the Psyche,* CW 8, pars. 142f.

distress, and being enlarged by the suffering of this conflict, is how we grow and mature. As Jung notes, "Suffering is not an illness; it is the normal counterpole to happiness."[90] Our goal is not happiness, which is evanescent and impossible to sustain; it is *meaning* which broadens us and carries us toward our destiny.

We recall the tendency to seek gurus, to transfer this need to the therapist. But Jung asserts a much more modest, and, in the end, more practical view of the dialogue of therapy:

> Analysis is not a method . . . of putting things into the patient that were not there before. It is better to renounce any attempt to give direction, and simply try to throw into relief everything that the analysis brings to light, so that the patient can see it clearly. . . . Anything he has not acquired himself he will not believe in the long run, and what he takes over from authority merely keeps him infantile. He should rather be put in a position to take his own life in hand.[91]

Taking back some control of our life, gaining a measure of autonomy in the face of the power of the environment, our fated familial and core complexes, and modestly creating a life—that is the goal of therapy. Does this mean that everyone should be in therapy, and all the time? Of course not. Any categorical attitude will be wrong for someone at any given moment. But consider how it is that one is supposed to know oneself when we admit that much of our lives are driven by the unconscious. And are we superior to others in our triumph over the ego's desire to hear what it wishes? Surely not.

So, figure out a better form of therapy than the committed, regular, sincere and deep conversation which can arise with an analytically-oriented therapist and do it. I believe that a therapeutic relationship, periodically renewed in the course of one's journey, is a profound opportunity for insight and growth. If the reader can find a mode of achieving this that works better, then do it. Failing that, we may be obliged to admit that the invention of analysis a century ago was, and remains, a pro-

---

[90] "General Problems of Psychotherapy," *The Practice of Psychotherapy,* CW 16, par. 179.
[91] "Crucial Points in Psychoanalysis," *Freud and Psychoanalysis,* CW 4, par. 643.

foundly moving approach to the desire of the soul to be met by the open attitude of consciousness. Out of such a meeting will be found healing amid the continuing suffering of life, new depth and purpose to one's journey and an ongoing renewal of the spirit.

To stop at behavioral change, as important as it is, or cognitive restructuring, liberating as it may be, and pharmacology, necessary as it sometimes becomes, betokens a failure of nerve and sells the soul very short indeed.

17
Fundamentalist Morality

As you may have discerned by now, I do not cotton much to fundamentalists of any kind. Not only do they fudge with contradictory facts, sluff over nuances which are always present, fall into simplistic and comforting answers, and abrogate the tension of opposites in favor of one side or the other, but there is also a terrified terrorist within who will put a gun to one's head to enforce agreement. Once we have agreed that there is a fundamentalist of some stripe in each of us, and that fundamentalism is fear-based, then we can begin to look at what is really fundamentalist morality.

The fundamentalists would have it that morality is a clear choice between good or evil, and of course they know which is which. While such discernments purportedly serve to make one feel secure on the side of good, and ostensibly clarify the nature of the bad, one finds a covert credo beneath all fundamentalist beliefs, though it may not be the one with which the true believers have identified.

If we define a morality as that which in the end proves to be most deeply, repeatedly true, then we may say that the fundamental reality which we all serve, whether we like it or not, is the principle Jung identified as compensation. Whatever is true to consciousness is compensated by its opposite in the unconscious. The more pious I am outwardly, the more violence lurks in my psyche, for I am the carrier of nature. Nature naturing is always seeking a dynamic tension of opposites. Consciousness, as we have seen, tends to privilege one value and exclude its contrary. That contrary does not go away; it is projected onto others, or it goes into the unconscious, only to emerge in some other time and place.

The more I identify with a value, the more one-sided becomes my orientation to reality. As that one-sided orientation excludes the range of possibilities, those rejected values are pathologized. In the life of the individual the excluded values will somaticize, express themselves in vigorous dream images, or be seen in projection.

In the classic film *The Blue Angel,* an arid, logic-bound professor happens by a cabaret and is smitten by the charms of a sultry chanteuse (Marlene Dietrich, of course). Identified with his logos powers of consciousness, and alienated from his primitive anima, he is enthralled by this feminine manifestation in the outer world. Just as his poor relationship to the inner life owned him, so the cabaret singer soon makes him her slave. His hold on his dignified, professorial persona swings to its opposite, pathetic servility.

Jung invokes the laws of Newtonian thermodynamics, especially the law that every action creates an equal and opposite reaction, and borrows the word *enantiodromia* from Heraclitus to identify the force that creates its opposite.

If compensation is the deepest truth in the end, then the injustices of consciousness are served by compensatory forces in the unconscious psyche. A woman whose ex-husband had abused her complained that he seemed to skate away free from consequences, always eluding responsibility: I pointed out that she did not have to wake up to him any more, but that he had to wake to his pained inner life always. "But he doesn't seem to care," she said. "No matter," I replied, "his psyche knows and suffers its aridity every day, a pain so great that he had to try to beat it out of his life by projecting it on to you. It is far better to suffer an injustice from another than to live it day in and day out, without escape."

We see the principle of compensation at work continuously in fairy tales, where story after story shows that the dominant attitude of consciousness has, through its one-sidedness, placed the kingdom in some jeopardy. The crops do not grow, the queen is barren, the king is dying, or there is some other indication of imbalance. Naturally consciousness would dismiss the problem, reject the opposing values and shun the forces—peasants, dwarfs, discharged soldiers, etc.—who in the end emerge as the agents of redemption.

In Grimm's "King Thrushbeard," for example, a haughty attitude is embodied in a young woman who judges everyone around her, rejects every suitor and is subsequently abducted by a beggar who brings her to sundry acts of servitude. Such "lowering" is familiar to us all, whether it manifest as depression, rejection by a loved one, or simply stumbling over our own best intentions. It is part of the fundamental morality of the soul that the high shall be brought low, the low exalted, and all things will abide not in stasis but in dynamic tension.

Snow-White's stepmother is a narcissistically wounded woman who constantly consults her mirror for reassurance that she is the fairest in the land. Narcissism is frequently a consequence of insufficient mirroring in early life, which occasions a gaping hole in one's sense of self. This emptiness is compensated by an urgent desire for affirmation from others. It is not that one is in love with oneself; rather, it is that when he or she stares into the mirror, nothing stares back, hence the urgency and the manipulation of others aimed at filling this unfillable hole. As the hole is forever empty, the need to control and colonize others is a constant.

On the other hand, Snow-White personifies an energy which establishes contact with the dwarfs—undeveloped, powerful sources—as well as an emergent animus attitude, the prince who kisses her awake, who in the end enable her to overthrow the legacy of deficiency. This pattern can be found in the person with insufficient mirroring who one day ceases to depend on others for self-worth, instead trusting the dormant powers within, given by nature to promote survival and, mayhap, spiritual abundance in the world.

The hole left by inadequate parental mirroring may only be healed by a leap of faith toward the resources within oneself. This faith, or trust in the healing powers of the unconscious, can lead to healing through the process of self-reflection. The emptiness of the narcissistic psyche obsessively seeks to be compensated by coercing positive mirroring from family, friends and therapists. Yet the healing compensation for the missing other can only be found by connecting with the inner powers we were all born with.

The fundamental morality of the cosmos, and of the individual human psyche, can offer no comfort, no predictability, to fundamentalists. The fundamental morality of the cosmos depends on bringing all values into play in a dynamic tension. Thus homophobia, for example, is a denial of one's fragile hold on one's own sexual identity. Single-minded evangelism is a privileging of one's personal complexes lest they be overthrown by the truth embodied in opposing values. The fundamental morality of the psyche suggests that the moment one is convinced that something is true, then the opposite is already at work in oneself. Holding this unsettling thought at bay by rationalized defensiveness of the conscious position only reinforces the surreptitious work of the shadow.

The psyche is forever presenting us with compensatory energies. As Freud was wont to say, people denied his theories by day and dreamt them at night. It may be disconcerting to the fundamentalist in each of us, but such a natural morality is the truly fundamental one. The wise move, then, would be always to look for the opposite in ourselves, in others, in our culture.

18
What is Real Beneath Reality?

Is the world a series of illusions, or *maya* as the Hindus called it, in which we participate with more or less awareness of their provisional nature? Is the old paradox valid—that we live in a dream, or are being dreamt by another? Is this world "God's play," as the Hindu metaphor would have it? When do we feel real, if ever, or most nearly real? When we are in pain? When we are in a reflexive, instinctual moment? When we are most detached from the flow and flux of everyday life and are reflective? When we are in the presence of the mystery, however idiosyncratically defined?

Paradoxically, Hamlet may seem more real to us today than the man who immortalized his dilemma. As Aristotle suggested in his *Poetics,* works of the imagination are often more real than events in history, for they partake of the universal; that is, they dramatize the archetypal in a way that historical particularities cannot.

While it is useful to reflect often on the illusions of progress for the same reasons we reflect on mortality—to keep things in perspective and to contain the investment of ego in outcomes—still it behooves us to think on when we are most real. We tend to think of selfhood as a goal out there which may in time be realized, more or less, with right effort, right conduct and so on. That the Self is an autonomous agent of change, of transformation, whose *telos* is its own fullest realization, I have no doubt. Yet those changes and teleologies may have virtually nothing to do with the self-ratifying desires of the ego.

Ask yourself, "When do I feel most real?" What comes up on the screen? All of us will have had moments in our lives when we felt whole or wholly present, or experienced a sense of well-being, an intuition of a higher order of reality. Such moments are transitory, alas, and cannot be summoned up by will or mind or right conduct, just as the person who seeks humility finds more and more that pride and one-sidedness push the goal further and further away.

Depth psychologists view symptoms as a vital key to the intentions of the Self, one's inner regulating center. Their very presence is evidence of the active, dynamic, autonomous nature of the Self, which day to day comments on how our life is being led. "Reading" such signals, which manifest most notably in dreams, is the thorny task of analysis. Such readings tell us much of the place and etiology of wounding, the countervalue which is to be honored, and the role of consciousness in support of the healing task.

To much of the therapeutic community, welcoming symptoms seems absurd or counterproductive, but to the psychodynamically oriented, symptoms are the critical road signs of our journey, exemplified by the Greek god Hermes, who crosses over from world to world in search of communion. All healing invokes Hermes, the god of crossings, for he bridges the known and the unknown and makes possible their reconciliation. If one were able to align one's conscious choices and attitudes with the teachings of our suffering, might one not then experience a sense of the real?

Jung has identified a third possibility for the experience of the real—the idea of vocation. As individuals, we are not meant to be well-balanced, sober servants of collective values. We are not meant to be sane, safe or similar. We are, each of us, meant to be different. A proper course of therapy does not make us better adjusted; it makes us more eccentric, a unique individual who serves a larger project than that of the ego or collective norms.

What Jung says on this subject bears repeating:

> What is it, in the end, that induces a man to go his own way and to rise out of unconscious identity with the mass as out of a swathing mist? Not necessity, for necessity comes to many, and they all take refuge in convention. Not moral decision, for nine times out of ten we decide for convention likewise. What is it, then, that inexorably tips the scales in favour of the *extra-ordinary*?
>
> It is what is commonly called *vocation:* an irrational factor that destines a man to emancipate himself from the herd and from its well-worn paths. True personality is always a vocation and puts its trust in it as in God, despite its being, as the ordinary man would say, only a personal feeling. But

vocation acts like a law of God from which there is no escape. The fact that many a man who goes his own way ends in ruin means nothing to one who has a vocation. He *must* obey his own law, as if it were a daemon whispering to him of new and wonderful paths. Anyone with a vocation hears the voice of the inner man: he is *called.*[92]

How revolutionary to our childhoods it would be if Jung's identification of vocation were taught as our *raison d'être*. It would give us all a task, a sense of personal summons, a dignity, a life-long mission. We would not be enjoined to pursue the delusory success which William James called "the bitch goddess."[93] We might find our proper path even more along the trail of ruin, through the savannas of suffering. Certainly Jesus did, to cite one rather well-know example. As Jung noted,

> Are we to understand the "imitation of Christ" in the sense that we should copy his life and, if I may use the expression, ape his stigmata; or in the deeper sense that we are to live our own proper lives as truly as he lived his in its individual uniqueness? It is no easy matter to live a life that is modelled on Christ's, but it is unspeakably harder to live one's own life as truly as Christ lived his.[94]

The shape and character of our vocation may change at different developmental stages. We have not just one life, but many lives to live, and in the course of however long we are privileged to live, many tasks, many vocations. Personality, or personhood as Jung might define it, is not found in adjustment to external expectations, but in serving one's calling in the context of our environment. This may bring one to an individual experience of being "misjudged, derided, tortured, and crucified."[95] No wonder vocation is so seldom served. And yet, and yet, something in us always knows better. Something in us, no matter how much we flee it, summons us. We may avoid it all our lives, but deep down, something knows. It knows us whether we wish to know it or not.

---

[92] "The Development of Personality," *The Development of Personality,* CW 17, pars. 299f.

[93] *The Varieties of Religious Experience,* p. 194

[94] "Psychotherapists Or the Clergy," *Psychology and Religion,* CW 11, par. 522.

[95] Ibid.

There is no escape from this knowing though much of contemporary Western culture is a flight from knowing what, inescapably, we already know.

The higher law which vocation embodies is the purposefulness of the cosmos, whose mystery may never be plumbed and which has little to do with the ego's desires. Jung says one *must* serve this higher law of personhood. The daemon is the god Hermes, crossing the boundaries between worlds to communicate to quotidian consciousness the intentions of the other world.

Of course there is a long process of discernment which must attend this summons. We hear many voices—the voices of complexes, the voices of culture, the mad voices. How do we know which ones come from Hermes? One should never make a major decision on the basis of a single dream, or a single event, or a single voice. If it is Hermes, he will call upon us again, and again, in dreams, in affect, in body, and in the intuitions which vouchsafe for a moment a vision of the whole. Discernment is critical to sorting through the sundry voices, and may only be achieved after careful sifting, including the ego's contribution of ethical considerations. In the end, a real life will have little to do with the plans of culture or ego, but rather will be shaped by what the gods have in mind.

We will be most nearly real when we serve our vocation. We will not be spared suffering, but we will be granted a deeply felt sense that our life is right, even when suffering isolation and rejection. That deeply felt inner sense of what is right for us, which Marie-Louise von Franz calls "the instinct of truth,"[96] is how we can find what it is we are to do with this precious and fragile gift of life and the transcendent reality we are summoned to serve. This sacrifice of the ego will constitute our greatest gift to the world. Jung writes,

Individuation cuts one off from personal conformity and hence from col-

---

[96] "One reacts rightly without knowing why, it flows through one and one does the right thing. . . . With the help of the instinct of truth, life goes on as a meaningful flow, as a manifestation of the Self." *(Alchemy: An Introduction to the Symbolism and the Psychology,* pp. 172f.)

lectivity. That is the guilt which the individual leaves behind for the world, that is the guilt he must endeavor to redeem. He must offer a ransom in place of himself, that is, he must bring forth values which are an equivalent substitute for his absence in the collective personal sphere.[97]

The sacrifice of collective acceptance, which individuation demands, is redeemed by our bringing a larger person back to the world, to our relationships and to our dialogue with mystery.

---

[97] "Adaptation, Individuation, Collectivity," *The Symbolic Life,* CW 18, par. 1095.

19
What Is Our True Duty?

What is our true, our highest, duty—to others, the values of the tribe, the family, to oneself? Is it to God, to a higher calling of some sort? This is the critical question of the second half of life. *What am I called to serve?*

If the question is not asked consciously, we will be possessed by something, some unconscious value, some complex, some adolescent rebellion which continues unabated. If we ask the question consciously, we will have to ask it periodically, at different stages of life. An answer valid for one stage may be oppressive in another. What will have focused one's goals in one part of life may prove to be irrelevant in another.

As we have seen in fairy tales, the "morality" served there is not a conventional morality, a struggle wherein good wins over evil. Rather the morality of folk and fairy tales is the morality of nature itself, the psychodynamic balance of opposites which, because the opposites are valued, serves wholeness as well as survival. In "The Goose Girl" and "The True Bride," both Grimm tales, one finds the metaphor of the true and false bride, namely, the spiritual value to which one is married. As the tales seek the psychodynamic balance of all values, there is, finally, no true or false value, simply opposing truths. However, in any given situation there is a stasis which has become neurotic through its privileging of one value or energy over another.

When we look intrapsychically, we ask, then, what value is true; that is, what is most useful for this stage or situation? The value true in one context may be false in another. As noted in the chapter on ambition, what is useful in the spring of life is delusory baggage in the second half. Ambition in youth is a necessary testing of one's capacities; ambition in the older person stems from unresolved identity needs. The Hermes capacity for theft of what one needs may be reprehensible in one context and a saving grace in another.

Thus, our duties are many, and our contexts variable. We may all agree that sometimes one's duty is to others, such as our children, and sometimes it is to ourselves as we struggle to preserve the integrity of our individuation. There was, however, a time, and not so long ago, when one's duty was to duty itself.

In the Victorian era, which created the core complexes which governed our grandparents who governed our parents who governed us, the need to find one's proper duty was urgent. This urgency was fueled by the cultural angst which derived from the erosion of the great Western myths and their sacred institutions. Feeling that the metaphysical rug had been pulled from beneath their tribal values, the Victorians sought to enthrone duty, moral action and value as the new religion.

The French Lieutenant's Woman, a novel by John Fowles, illustrates this vision of duty for those who lived a century earlier. Charles Smithson is a man of his age, yearning for meaning, obliged to take the new science seriously. He is a geologist who seeks clues to the oldest of the earth's secrets. His betrothed is Ernestina ("little earnest"). Charles meets Sarah Woodruff who has fallen into disrepute because of her affair with a French lieutenant who abandoned her. The first time Charles sees her, she stands pining, looking out over a cold sea. He is immediately smitten. Ernestina is described as pretty, Sarah as deep. Their normative reference is a Mrs. Poutenary whose two obsessions are dirt and immortality, that is, moral order and piety. As such, these women represent not only the three persona roles available to women of the time, but three anima manifestations for Charles.

When we recall that the use of the word "leg" was considered obscene, and euphemistically replaced by "limb," that chairs were to have their limbs "fully skirted," and that Lady Gough, the social arbiter of her class, dictated that only married couples, such as the Brownings, should be placed side by side, male and female, in bookshelves, then we know that these folks lived in a world closely governed by prescriptive morality. One Victorian worthy dressed her goldfish, another left money in her will to clothe the snowmen of Paris; bulls were often called "gentlemen cows," and so on. John Ruskin, having believed women looked as pristine as the statues at the British Museum, was so shocked at the first and only sight of his wife's pubic hair that he withdrew in horror and never touched her throughout their marriage. (I have made none of this up. We

live in a "fallen, degenerate" society, and have no idea how far we have
fallen from just a short while ago.)

Underneath this Victorian obsession with dirt, sex and alien ideas, was
an anxiety about the floor slipping away from them. Our recent obser-
vance of millennial paranoias is a similar measure of how free-floating
anxiety attaches itself to numinous ideas—even a total abstraction such
as the year 2000—and projects apocalyptic fantasies. As Fowles writes,

> They sensed that current accounts of the world were inadequate; that they
> had allowed their windows on reality to become smeared by convention,
> religion, social stagnation; in short, that they had things to discover, and
> that the discovery was of the utmost importance to the future of man.[98]

Charles is betrothed to Ernestina, yet obsessed with Sarah. We must
recall that an engagement in the Victorian era had the weight of a contract, the abrogation of which entailed enormous legal and social reper-
cussions. Sadly, the most natural of things, the sexual question, became a
complex. Ernestina, no doubt on the advice of her mother, had, according
to Fowles,

> evolved a kind of private commandment—those inaudible words were
> simply "I must not"—whenever the physical female implications of her
> body, sexual, menstrual, parturitional, tried to force an entry into her con-
> sciousness. But though one may keep the wolves from one's door, they
> still howl out there in the darkness. Ernestina wanted a husband, wanted
> Charles to be that husband, wanted children, but the payment she vaguely
> divined she would have to pay for them seemed excessive. . . . She some-
> times wondered why God had permitted such a bestial version of Duty to
> spoil an innocent longing.[99]

Was Ernestina born with these ideas? Did she suffer such an estrangement from the good juices of her own body at birth, and from the
God who created them? Her duty lay before her like a crucifixion—a
complexed, repressed nature, a strong superego demand, a deep yearning
and the weight of indecision. (Lest we judge our ancestors, smirk at their
prudery in this age of sexual overload, let us acknowledge that the same

---

[98] *The French Lieutenant's Woman,* p. 44.
[99] Ibid., p. 29.

splits still haunt us, else there would be no pornography, prostitution, frigidity, nonbiological impotence, virgin-whore split, inhibited sexual desire and the like. Poor Ernestina; poor Victorians; poor us).

Charles's call to duty is expressed through his seriousness, his commitment to the new sciences, to his betrothed, and to being a decent man. And yet, and yet, there was that terrible summons of the blood which Sarah evoked. As for Sarah, she had given her heart to a man who had deserted her. But rather than see her as the victim, we learn that she deliberately sacrificed herself and her reputation.

> I did it so that I would never be the same again. I did it so that people *should* point at me, *should* say, there walks the French Lieutenant's whore. . . . There was a kind of suicide. An act of despair. . . . What has kept me alive is my shame. . . . Sometimes I pity them. I think I have a freedom they cannot understand.[100]

Sarah has evoked the perverse freedom of dying unto a life which is not hers, even without the promise of some place to which she has to move to find a life which *is* hers.

So, we have the three: Ernestina, the very best product of collective culture; Sarah in existential revolt; and Charles, the thoroughly modern Victorian man, caught between them. Even in the realm of his intellectual/spiritual pursuit of the wonders which science opens, Charles is imprisoned. His geological research, not unlike that of the testimonies of depth psychology, biology and social philosophy, demonstrates to him that we are less and less free, more and more predetermined. Charles knows only a fraction of what we know now, the genetic programming we all enact, the social Darwinism which shows how much we are a product of culture and class, the great revolution of Freud who demonstrated the effect of unconscious forces on behavior and history itself. In search of freedom, he encounters more and more prisons. No wonder Dostoyevsky, in *Notes from Underground* (1863), worried that humanity was being reduced to the anonymity and predictability of a piano key, played upon by unknown, indifferent forces. As Fowles has it, Charles discovers, "In that silent Dorset night, reason and science dissolved; life

---

[100] Ibid., p. 142.

was a dark machine, a sinister astrology, a verdict at birth and without appeal, a zero over all. . . . He had never felt less free."[101]

While the story is told by watching over the shoulder of Charles, the real protagonist is Sarah. Charles, having 'fessed up to Ernestina, is in disgrace, and Sarah disappears. He follows her for years and finally tracks her down. A happy ending, right? Fowles, a thoroughly postmodern novelist, gives the reader three possible endings.

The Victorian ending is most accessible. Charles sees the futility of his doomed love, marries Ernestina, inherits the business, sires seven children who become the next generation of keepers of the kingdom. The modern ending shows Charles pursuing Sarah to the ends of the earth, whereupon they have brief, furtive, passionate sex, and then "the radioactivity of guilt crept through his nerves and veins."[102] Whereupon Sarah walks away, and Charles, the devastated Victorian, is left to grief and confusion. As Charles understands his dilemma, "You stay in prison, what your time calls duty, honor, self-respect, and you are comfortably safe. Or you are free and you are crucified."[103]

One or other of the above two scenarios has been lived out by many of us. Some of us have lived them both.

In the context of his time, Charles has little choice. He knew that he could not claim that Ernestina was his love, and yet respectability meant an acceptable identity, even though he felt deeply that "the pursuit of money was an insufficient purpose in life," and that what lay before him was the "vast plain of tedium—and unlike the famous pilgrim, he saw only Duty and Humiliation down there below—most certainly not Happiness or Progress."[104]

The third ending Fowles supplies shows Sarah having gone off to become the protomodern woman, the one who pursues her own desires. She joins a group around the poet Dante Gabriel Rossetti, which for the time was a very radical a move. In this ending to the novel, when Charles

---

[101] Ibid., p. 188.
[102] Ibid., p. 275.
[103] Ibid., p. 284.
[104] Ibid., pp. 228, 233.

finally tracks Sarah down, she spurns his sincere offer of marriage. When he asks if she is in love with another, she replies:

> The rival you both share is myself. . . . I do not wish to marry because of my past which habituated me to loneliness. . . . I do not wish to share my life. I wish to be what I am, not what a husband, however kind, however indulgent, must expect me to become. . . . I never expected to be happy in life. Yet I find myself happy. . . . I have varied and congenial work. . . . I am admitted to the daily conversation of genius.[105]

The idea of individuation was not available to the citizens of that generation. Ernestina is wholly a prisoner of the "catatonia of convention."[106] Charles is crucified between duty on the one hand and passion on the other. Sarah has undertaken the ultimate risk of being who she is, following her soul's summons, but at the cost of social suicide. She is seeking the integration of the animus—unthinkable for Ernestina and beyond the comprehension of well-intended Charles, but certainly a psychologically healthy pursuit for women in our own time.

To what then is our duty? To others? To our complexes? To individuation? What does individuation mean, really? May it not be simply an excuse for transitory and/or transitional madness, for self-indulgence? Do not most of us live the public life of Ernestina, suffer the bad dreams of Charles, and still yearn for the costly freedom of Sarah?

What is our duty to self and others? How are we to manage the competing claims of fidelity to relationships and summons to soul? These are the questions, part and parcel of individuation, that are to be lived, and continuously suffered, in the second half of life. The unconscious path of familiarity dooms one to living superficially. The conscious path of individuation means accepting the potentially creative tension of opposites, which inevitably involves a degree of crucifixion. To what do we owe our highest duty?

---

[105] Ibid., pp. 252f.
[106] Ibid., p. 300.

20
The Camp of Concentrated Shadow Work

Residence in the camp of concentrated shadow work is the moral consequence of becoming conscious in the second half of life. The chief fantasy most of us served as we left our parents was that we would be decent, moral beings, that we would not hurt others, least of all our children. Who could have thought that just by being who we were, we would
hurt our children, our mate and ourselves?

A useful basket definition of the shadow is: that which I do not wish
to be, that within myself with which I least desire to associate, that which
I find frightening, anarchic and threatening to my self-image. No small
portion of Freud's imaginative genius was to write *The Psychopathology
of Everyday Life*. One does not have to go to a mental asylum, he concluded, to see the interruptive influence of the unconscious. While Jung,
in his research into the implications of the Word Association Experiment, was shortly to describe those autonomous interferences as complexes, Freud was profound in his intuition that the work with our for-
bidden life begins with the work of our daily life.

Our understanding of shadow, however, must be broad enough to
transcend the common assumption that the word is synonymous with
evil. Certainly anger and sexuality are shadow issues, given their complexed character for our culture. And why are they so full of that excess
energy which denotes a complex? Most likely because both anger and
sexuality are autonomous energies, forces which have the power to
overthrow the collective and the dictates of ego consciousness, and might
lead one to nonrational experience. At the same time, such energies as
spontaneity and creativity are also shadow-laden, for they represent powerful threats to the ego's longing for the safe and familiar.

One of the ways in which one can begin to become conscious of the
personal shadow is to consult one's partner or closest friends. Each of
them can quickly supply us with an agenda of our shadow work, just as
we might prepare such a list for them. Another way to begin the neces-

sary work is to maintain a journal on issues such as the following:

1) When Jung said that the greatest burden of the child is the unlived life of the parent, he was pointing toward the power of that repressed material to set the tone and the agenda for our own lives. In general, we seek to replicate those experiences, compensate for them or heal them, or some combination thereof. Thus we are challenged to address, again and again (for what comes up first is not always reliable and never really enough), these questions:

—In what way am I carrying the unlived life of my parent?

—Where am I stuck, blocked, as my parent was blocked?

—Where am I caught in a compensation which, though it may be productive for me and others, shackles me to the consequences of someone else's life?

No matter how conscious we may be, we are all caught in one of these ways. The subtlety of the results is staggering. Our primal experiences, and the complexes attending them, are shape-changers that surprise us in ever new venues, with ever new appearances, but with the same old outcomes, realized only in the backdraft of reflection.

2) How am I perpetuating the world view, the strategies, the behaviors, of my mother? Of my father? Where do they show up, like unwelcome flashes in the mirror which show the parent's face shining through ours, or where one finds one's relationship to one's children not unlike the relationship one had to one's parent, or when the intimate relationship seems fatally wounded by inescapable and familiar patterns? Such shadow work is humiliating, but it is necessary to labor in such sweatshops of the soul before one can find the freedom to move elsewhere.

3) Where is the spontaneous child we once were? None of us has a ghost of a chance of living all the diverse dimensions of our psychic spectrum, our potential. When one considers the narrow tribal gate through which all children are obliged to pass, the range of choices is still further limited.

The cruel hoax of "retirement" is that when one is finally free to pursue one's interest, to experience one's golden years, little has been rendered conscious, or permissible, in order to make such abundant life possible.

4) Where is the unlived life which haunts, or summons, or intimidates you? We have all been called to spiritual greatness. Not the greatness of worldly standard, but the largeness of individuation, the vocation to be who we are, in the peculiar fashion the psyche demands, at whatever cost may be exacted by the collective. Somewhere, deep inside of each of us, is the knowing which knows us, that mystery which seeks us, desires realization through us. What a defilement of our calling it is to live the lesser life. We may be frightened by the scope of such calling, but it is even more frightening to have stayed stuck in a life of no consequence, of no contribution. Fear of the call is a good fear, for it reduces the other fears to their lesser claim on us.

5) Where am I asking others to take responsibility for my life? Let's face it—we would all love to be taken care of. We all are recovering children who project the dynamics of the intrapsychic parent onto an institution, an ideology, and most commonly onto intimate relationships. Growing up is ever more difficult because it requires letting go of old expectations of rescue and redemption. We are it; this is it; this is as good as it gets, and we better deal with it.

6) Each of us lives, in Sartre's phrase, in *mauvaise foi* (bad faith), and are summoned to live in *bonne foi* (good faith). We live in bad faith whenever we betray our calling, whenever, in the second half of life, we do not find the wherewithal to take on the project of growing up. The first half of life is a bloody blundering, a great mistake, but necessary and worthy. One has to live it in order to gain enough ego strength to reflect upon it and learn what must be learned from the debacle of the past. One has to live it to form character.

Living in good faith does not, of course, spare us suffering, mistakes, death and dissolution; however, it means that one has a sense of the rightness of one's journey, with or without the agreement of others.

7) Recall that the poet Mary Oliver arrived at the point where she concluded, "I don't want to end up simply having visited this world."[107] Visitors we are; tourists we are; but we wish to have mattered, somehow. To this end, we have to ask the question: What part of yourself do you

---

[107] Above, p. 80.

need to get to know better in order to feel more complete, to have not simply been a visitor here? What agenda is now demanding attention? What growing up do we have to achieve? What security, old identity, relationship, pathology do we need to leave behind?

Such questions are the sort which one is obliged to ask, suffer and develop provisional responses to over the course of the second half of life. As Rilke observed, we are not yet ready to live the answers.[108] But we bloody well must live the right questions. If we do, we may someday live into the answers, the place where choice and destiny have been intending to meet since before we were born. Such labor in the camp of concentrated shadow work is critical to the enlargement of soul, relinquishment of false identities, unburdening of relationships, and the recovery of personal integrity.

---

[108] *Letters to a Young Poet,* p. 35.

21
Sad Stories of the Death of Kings

> Nothing that is worth doing can be achieved in our lifetime;
> therefore we must be saved by hope. Nothing which is true or
> beautiful or good makes complete sense in any immediate contest
> of history; therefore, we must be saved by faith. Nothing we ever
> do, however virtuous, can be accomplished alone; therefore, we
> must be saved by love.
>
> —Reinhold Niebuhr, *The Children of Light.*

In one of the most moving of all of Shakespeare's scenes, Richard II, having lost the critical battle, his throne, his autonomy, as has happened to most of us, summons his comrade soldiers to the campfire and says,

> . . . what can we bequeath
> Save our deposed bodies to the ground? . . .
> And nothing can we call our own but death
> And that small model of the barren earth
> Which serves as paste and cover to our bones.
> For God's sake, let us sit upon the ground
> And tell sad stories of the death of kings . . .
> . . . for within the hollow crown
> That rounds the mortal temples of a king
> Keeps Death his court and there the antic sits,
> Scoffing his state and grinning at his pomp . . .
> Infusing him with self and vain conceit,
> As if this flesh which walls about our life
> Were brass impregnable . . .
> . . . subjected thus,
> How can you say to me, I am a king?[109]

One of the chief fantasies of the first half of life is that of accomplishment, necessary accomplishment, without which we would not achieve an ego identity in the world. But no one who has reached the second half of life has not had to live through profound disappointment,

---

[109] *Richard II*, act 3, scene 2, lines 149ff.

defeat and humiliations of one sort or another.

Our hearts are broken many, many times, by outer losses and by very personal defeats. Shakespeare dramatizes with great sympathy how proud Richard has finally come to earth, not only in political defeat, but through the recollection of his mortality, the stunning reminder of the fragility of that "paste and cover to our bones." No wonder depression is endemic to the retired, the elderly, the dispossessed, those for whom the festival of losses is everyday. No wonder there's so much Prozac, booze and early, unexplained death. The world breaks our bloody heart, and each chamber screams aloud in protest.

But theologian Niebuhr's reminder, quoted above, of the paradox of loss and gain is useful. I heard Martin Luther King speak in 1965, just before he was murdered. He was asked when he thought America's racial problem might be transcended and he replied that it would take at least until 2000. I recall that at the time, naively, I thought how impossibly long, how far away that day is. Like the geniuses who created computers and did not think that the calendar might roll over into a new century rather soon, I naively considered 2000 to be an infinity away, and I was gravely disappointed at Dr. King's prediction.

Today I know that bigotry will never be erased because there will always be ignorant and frightened people. They will continue to project their fears, their unconscious splits, onto others and disown their own shadow. But does this mean that the opposition to bigotry is to be suspended, or that one should not oppose it everywhere, through education, political action and personal example—of course not. Nothing worth doing, Niebuhr reminds, will be achieved in our lifetime. And it will never be achieved, ever, if we do not contribute our small part. Again, the ego's fantasy of control and sovereignty is overthrown in favor of the lesser comfort of hope. Hope is an aspiration of the spirit, and that to which we aspire will not only be the framer of our energies but a measure of our values as well. We may even hope for the fulfillment of Shelley's assertion that we are to "hope until hope creates from its own wreck the thing it contemplates."[110] Such hope is never defeated, for it is

---

[110] "Prometheus Unbound," line 806, in Untermeyer, ed., *A Concise Treasury*, p. 71.

an expression of the essence of our soul.

Moreover, the incompleteness of our lives, the always unfinished journey, makes frustration and defeat inevitable. And in any given historical setting, no justice is final, no vindication unequivocal, no cause permanently achieved. The long view of history must be an expression of faith, tempered by realism and pragmatism rather than cynicism. What little drop we contribute to the ocean, whatever spark we contribute to the bonfire, is nonetheless the needed part of the whole. Individuation itself is obscure, its goals uncertain, and yet, as the carrier of the purposes of nature, or of the gods, it is the means through which the universe is progressively incarnated. While we may not believe in the doctrine of progress, as did our Victorian antecedents, we may nonetheless see history as a progressive unfolding of a great drama of which the individual is a necessary part. This faith, as it were, is not professing certainty or clarity, merely an openness to the possibility of a meaning which transcends not only our personal defeats but which embraces us.

Because *love* is so highly sentimentalized in popular culture, one is loath to even use the word. But what Niebuhr suggests is that we are all in this together, that the divine is present even in the defeats, that the angel of meaning flutters over the bitterest of losses, and that it is our capacity to bear witness to these paradoxes which is redemptive.

Love, as Niebuhr uses it, is a quality of soul which embraces the world, embraces our experience, painful as it may prove, and affirms it. Such an energy is tenacious and allows one to hold one's head up even when humiliated. Richard II was of course right. None of us remains a king for very long. Our pompous monarchism must cause peals of laughter among the gods. But even the gods may respect that species which is capable of hope, faith and love—despite all the reasons why such emotions, such attitudes, are impossible. Edward Hirsch concludes,

> What is this emptiness, the earth,
> but a black sea pulsing without Eros
> under infinitely dead starry spaces?
> Love alone can redeem our universe.[111]

---

[111] "Giacomo Leopardi," in *On Love*, p. 31.

So, as Shakespeare's Richard muses, we are here but awhile before antic Death removes our crown. Notwithstanding, that same Stratford man, during the plague years of the 1590's, when the theaters were closed and he was out of work, wrote over one hundred and fifty sonnets to his beloved "dark ladie." The common thread which runs through those sonnets, in the context of the tumbrels carrying the dead, cart-load after cart-load, to the dumping ground, was that something transcended death after all. It was not the established religion, with its promise of an afterlife. It was love, sacred and profane. And it was love as transfigured by the imagination, which survives even its creators. Hirsch observes:

> For man and woman, the days pass into years
> and the body is a grave filled with time.
> We are drowning. All that rescues us is love.[112]

Over and over, sonnet after sonnet, Shakespeare plaintively proclaims to his beloved that soon they, too, will die, yet the verse he has written will make them both immortal. He is right, partly, for we still celebrate their love through these incarnations of the imagination. Yet the cold, dark universe veers toward us, and someday there will there be no one who remembers Shakespeare, nor reads the Queen's English, nor even exists in any present shape or form. We are a body, and the body is a grave filled with time, in which we are decomposing. Is it not our ultimate delusion that in some way we will survive, even with such imaginative capacities as our Shakespeare?

So, Shakespeare now is dead, and so too his "dark ladie," and Mr. W.H., to whom he dedicated his verse. Yet they still live, not only in the realm of the imaginal, but in the images of our desire. Love may not prevail, or even survive, but it is priceless in the course of our troubled sojourn on this spinning planet. The capacity to love, in the face of the absurdity of our ends, permits us to live an enlarged life. Such a life will not be measured by its successes, but by the quality of its yearning.

---

[112] "Heinrich Heine," ibid., p. 33.

22
Today Nothing Happened

On the day that the Bastille fell, King Louis XVI of France wrote in his journal: *"Rien."* (Nothing)

23
Reading the World

Once, I had been teaching a class on the Buddhist perspective that suffering is caused by the fantasy of control, and since we are not really in control of very much at all, our suffering can only increase. Classical Buddhism is in fact more a psychology than a religion, a psychology which seeks the management of angst by, paradoxically, giving over to it. The more anxious one is, the more one is asked to relinquish the thought of conquering anxiety. This letting go of a fantasy allows one to dissipate the emotion while surrendering to it.

Since I had an appointment in another city, I carried my car keys with me to class, to save the five minutes it would take to return to the office to fetch them. After class, I raced to the parking lot and found that my keys were missing. My angst ratcheted up several notches. I spent the entire day frustrated, angry and yes, anxious, looking for those keys. The rational guide posts, the lost and found department, the campus police, were unhelpful. Finally, at the end of the day I was phoned by someone who had picked them up, carried them around all day in his pocket, and hours later decided to do something about it. By then I had gotten the message. What my head had been teaching, my heart had not grasped. For the saving of five minutes, in order to be more in control of my commute, I lost the appointment and the whole day. Since that time, I have had even greater respect for the Buddhist perspective. The lesson was learned the hard way, the usual way we learn.

This lesson is a rather obvious reading of the reality of the Tao beneath the surface. We pay attention to our dreams because we need to intuit the Tao. The focus of consciousness is often quite remote from what is coursing beneath the surface.

It is interesting to note that as children we often learned to read the world around us, and often misread it, as statements about ourselves. So-called primitive civilizations read the changes in the natural world as signs and omens, and often fell into magical thinking, in which there is an insufficient differentiation of objective and subjective reality. However, those predecessors lived still in the symbolic world, that is, where nature was still soul-full and not denuded of deeper values. Jung observed in his autobiography that the attainment of worldly goals were meaningless unless one lived the symbolic life. Living the symbolic life means that one has a sense of participation in a divine drama, an intuited connection to the forces which move nature and stir the blood. Whoever does not have such a sense is condemned to a banal existence, prey to fads, addictions, manias and progressive self-alienation.

I was once told by a physician that her chief encounter with depth had occurred one day when she realized that every relationship she had ever had had unfolded in rather much the same fashion. In her case, it was a pattern of disappointment and abandonment. Only when she grasped this most obvious of facts was she able to move from a sterile rationality to the perception of a prescient presence working in her life. If there could be such invisible forces shaping her fate, altering her destiny, making her choices for her, then there was reason to learn to respect what was invisible and pay closer attention to movements below the surface. When Jung said that a neurosis was an offended god, he was evoking those deep currents. Our violation of them, repression of them, projection of them, moves us out of relationship to the divine. The gods will not easily brook such injury; they retaliate through symptoms, interruptions and synchronistic accidents. For the want of five minutes I lost a day; there was a message there.

While identifying and interpreting patterns is profoundly helpful in making course corrections, it is sometimes very difficult to understand or intuit the directions the soul would prefer. How do we know? When do we trust an intuition? All of us have acted on what we thought was good intuitive evidence and been profoundly wrong. Do not go to the race track full of intuitions. Some of my best decisions derived from intuitive flashes, when the world seemed clear, and a certain choice meaningful. Yet some of my worst decisions also derived from intuitive flashes— when the world seemed clear, and a certain choice meaningful.

Reading the world obliges discernment. Discernment, as we have seen requires differentiation, sorting and sifting. The sorting and sifting motif is common in fairy tales, where the hero or heroine has to pick lice from fur, separate grains from chaff and so on. The implication seems to be that such sifting and sorting requires time, humility and patience until the right, or better, the necessary, appears. Few of us wish patience as a virtue these days. As powerful as dreams may be, any given dream may reflect only one side of a dilemma. The next night, or the next month, the value of its opposite will weigh in. It is the sign of the immature mind, of which we all have much experience, that it wishes to quickly grab one side of the dilemma and cling to it in the interests of assuaging the current anxiety of the ego. Each of us has inside an anxious fundamentalist who will take over when we are most stressed, most hurried, least determined to stick something out.

But the messages are everywhere, at all times. Consider when we do not know what we want to do. Remember that great discernment game, "Eenie, meenie, meinie, mo . . . ?" Recall how we added various coda to the outcome so as to flip the choice to its opposite. The addition of such coda tells us that we knew what we wanted to choose in the first place.

It is not unlike Aristophanes' comedy, *The Frogs*, written twenty-five centuries ago. Athens, having lost its visionaries, sends Heracles to Hades to bargain with the lower powers to retrieve a tragedian. As a comic figure he bumbles about, seeking to evaluate one over another. When at last he cannot decide, the goddess Athena appears and tells him with stunning simplicity that he should choose the one in which his heart delights. Heracles worships all the tragedians, but loves one, and his choice is abundantly clear.

Such a tumble into knowing what one already knows is similarly personified in Solomon's decision to split the contended baby in half. The real mother quickly manifests. From "Eenie, meenie, meinie . . ." to Solomon is a reminder that we always know, somewhere inside, what is right for us. We may fear to know what we know, so its costliness persuades ego to seek a thousand evasions; thus we dissemble, procrastinate, project onto others.

As an analyst, I am always aware that something inside that person knows. Often that knowing turns up in an initial dream or a sudden outburst. But it may take years for that knowing to percolate upward through the resistant sediment, years for the ego to gain sufficient strength to act upon what it desires. During that time, often terribly resistant complexes will have to be fought, not unlike the voyage of the mythic hero who must defeat beast after beast guarding the treasure. Those beasts, fears mostly, are parts of us. Not everyone defeats them; sometimes the beast of fear drives the person out of therapy into the arms of replicative history. Even so, that repetitive history is itself one of the profound clues that a pattern is being generated from an unknown source. It takes strength, humility or desperation, or all of these, to look long and hard at our patterns to discern the meaning they hold for us.

There is an essay by Jung called "The Spirit Mercurius," in which he pays particular attention to one of the Grimm tales, "The Spirit in the Bottle."[113] A youth, while walking in the forest, comes upon an oak which summons him. He finds a bottle with a voice that asks for release. The youth dutifully, perhaps naively, releases the spirit who grows into a giant who identifies himself as Hermes, the trickster god, or Mercurius. Mercurius then threatens to kill the youth. In such fashion are we all imperiled in the face of archetypal forces. But the youth, a true Dummling, tricks the trickster back into the bottle. This time, in return for release, the spirit offers a deal which includes the power to heal. At story's end, the youth is in a position to call upon powers which had earlier been too dangerous for him.

Jung's reading of this story suggests that the forest is symbolic of the unconscious, the oak the potential for individuation, and the mercurial spirit the powers of the unconscious which, if approached naively, can be destructive, but productive if treated with respect by a grounded ego. Jung notes that there are five stages which cultures go through, and likewise individuals, in the maturation process toward consciousness.

In stage one the voice of Mercurius remains unconscious and is simply projected onto the object, in this case the oak tree. In stage two a separation of subject (youth) and object (Mercurius) is experienced. In stage three the evil which the energy may embody is identified with the object "out there." In stage four the autonomy of that energy out there is now

---

[113] *Alchemical Studies,* CW 13, pars. 239ff.

suffered. In stage five, the energy of Mercurius is experienced as something within the subject, the youth.

Translating this into everyday terms, we see patterns unfold in the course of our lives, patterns which reflect individual history. As long as we remain unconscious of these inner sources, we project them onto the outer world. We may blame our parents, or the game stacked against us, or our partners. We have little sense of the difference between the projective identifications we live over and over, and their origin within us. In time, we begin to recognize that the enemy, so to speak, and therefore the deliverer as well, is within. We recognize that the energies we have projected onto the world derive from inner scenarios, that we are the makers of our world, and that the whole of the second half of life stands as a summons to consciousness. This means that what is wrong in my life is in me; what is repetitively wounding is in me; what is healing in my life is in me. As obvious as this may sound, in daily life such a recognition is as profound as it is difficult to achieve.

The clues are everywhere. Under our feet. In our relationship patterns. In the perceptions of those who know us best. Everywhere, and we do not see them until we are forced to. Think of Oedipus as the prototype. The omens announced, the prophecies declared, and he walks right into each blind alley. Then, blinded by all he has seen, he is humbled and comes at last to know himself fully. Though in exile and ruin, the gods bless him for this humble homecoming.

The world in which we live is filled with ubiquitous messages. Can we begin to read that world truly? Can we bear the blessing of the gods which comes from being responsible for our lives, the humbling which occurs in our seeing ourselves in the mirror, the liberating insights which bind us to ever deeper acknowledgments of accountability?

24
The Complexity of Relationships

I have found when lecturing in North America and Europe that no matter what the ostensible topic, more questions are asked about relationships than anything else. The questions always come around to relationship. On the one hand is the tautological observation that relationships are so important because they are so important. On the other hand, we may be drawn to conclude that perhaps there is something of an overvaluation of relationship, especially given the urgency of tone which accompanies such questions. Indeed, on this day in December 1999, I cannot even turn on my internet server without being invited to find a date for the coming millennium celebrations.

When we recall the fragility of our condition, that life begins with a profound and traumatic separation from which we never fully recover, that the mythology of the Fall stands at the beginning of our Western story, and that our dependence in childhood is total and angst-ridden, we get some clue as to how important relationships might be to us.

The imprinted imago of self and other which derives from earliest experience is deep-rooted and colors all subsequent relationships, especially intimate ones. Whenever we enter a new relationship, the present moment is flooded with the past. Such core perceptions as whether one feels valued or not, whether the world will meet us half way, whether the other is trustworthy or hurtful—all of these original experiences are laden with psychic energy and have an autonomy in proportion to their primacy and internalization before the age of reason, reflection and comparative frames of reference.

Considering how intimacy evokes such primordial imagos, how it floods the present with the dynamics of the past, and transfers the fantasy of healing and nurturance to the other, it is a wonder that any relationship can work at all, so burdened are they by the weight of personal history.

Usually when I talk like this people nod grudging assent, for they can begin to see such patterns in the history of their relationships, but they also show some resentment. To reflect on the problematics of relationship is to confront our omnipotent fantasies and to move closer to conscious relinquishment of our archetypal agendas; it forces us to start facing the limits of our condition.

There is evidence that people who have relationships tend to live longer and enjoy better physical and emotional health.[114] Yet it is also true that our pathology mainly derives from fleeing our essential aloneness. Even the best relationship can provide only a very small fraction of what one unconsciously seeks from the other. That is as good as it gets. But the urgency of the search for the magical other, the one who will take care of us, protect us, nurture us, spare us the rigors of our own journey, shows how fragile our condition really is.

We also know that our psychologies and our theologies are profoundly colored by the imprint of our primal relationships. Those who experienced the world as insufficiently there for them will have a greater need for closure, for reassurance from friends and loved ones, thus will often go out of their way to make relationship happen, for good or ill. Those who experienced the primal relationships as flooding their boundaries are more likely to avoid intimacy, maintain space in relationships, hedge on commitment or be highly selective in their friendships. Each floods the relational field with the dynamics of long ago and far away. Naturally, we all have experiences other than the first ones, but none have the staying power of those initial paradigms.

When we also realize that each person in a relationship brings to it a plethora of charged imagos, or complexes, which are active and forever being imposed on the interactive space, that mother and father are always there, silently gliding through the back rooms of our souls, and that the fantasy of primal reconnection resides archetypally in our psyche, then we understand why harmonious relationships are nearly impossible.

In the second half of life, we are obliged to sort out the utility of relationship while simultaneously defining its limits. Mature relationship will offer companionship, perhaps sexual intimacy, sometimes validation

---

[114] "Eight major community based studies, conducted between 1979 and 1994, showed that people who perceived themselves as socially isolated were two to five times more at risk for premature death from all causes." (*The Houston Chronicle,* May 25, 1998)

and support. But the chief service of a mature relationship is to provide us with the dialectic of otherness which is the requisite of personal growth. That is, rather than be a clone of our values, making us feel good about our narrow vision of the world, *the otherness of the other forces us to confront otherness.* Such a confrontation engenders a psychological dialectic which enlarges us through the experience of the opposites.

In the earlier chapter on fundamentalism, we saw how tempting it is to fasten on a single truth, to exclude alternative values in order to feel secure. Genuine relationship denies such security, forcing us to grow through understanding the values of the other. Just as our so-called enemies, or bad experiences, cause us to grow most, so our intimate relationships will thrive when we are able to value the enlargement which occurs from such interaction.

In youth, we are so insecure that we need others to confirm our shaky hold on reality. The insecure tend to band together to reinforce each other. Maturity, however, requires that we accept the largeness of our journey, and understand that we journey alone. What an astonishing thing it is, to be here, to be conscious, to feel the movement of eternal energies coursing through us, to intimate from time to time the high calling of personhood, the vocation of growth in service to the mystery which each of us embodies.

If one does not become the eccentric, unique, one-of-a-kind person he or she was meant to be, then a violation of some large purpose of the cosmos has occurred. Individuation is not self-absorption, narcissism or self-interest. On the contrary, individuation is a humbling task to serve what our deepest nature asks of us. For some it will be a path which brings public recognition, for others suffering and public calumny, for others still, private epiphanies never seen by anyone else. Any relationship which prevents or inhibits such a vocation is harmful and regressive.

In relinquishing the old agenda, we make room for something even richer. One may find a growing familiarity, even comfort, with being oneself, without apology or need for validation from others. When we are able to value being who we are—different, fractious, developing in ever new ways—then we really have something to share with others. The chief gift of relationship is the obligation to grow, which in turn serves the relationship by relieving it of the impossible demands of childhood.

We can best serve humankind by bringing our absolutely individualized fragment of life force to it. We will find better relationships when we ask less of them. We may even find them more comfortable as they become less predictable. This ambiguity is intolerable to the young, but a solid achievement for those who over the years have gained a relationship to themselves, a relationship which will survive no matter the outer vicissitudes. From the perspective of one's own hard-won reality, one can easily risk friendship and communication in terms of who one is.

There are three major issues that a person seeking to be mature and responsible must address in the context of relationships:

1) The level of dependence between the partners in a relationship tends to foster routinized expectations and behavior. Such patterns constrict the developmental potential of both parties. Thus, the moral question obliged of each is, *What am I asking of the other that I ought to ask of myself?* This question emphasizes the ethical obligation to assist the other by imposing less of one's own baggage upon him or her.

2) The inability to tolerate the differentness of the other results in controlling behaviors, passive-aggressive manipulation and sometimes outright warfare. Our task is to realize that the source of our intolerance is within ourselves, in our insufficiently developed sense of identity. Therapists who work with couples shudder when they see the controlling behaviors of the less conscious partner. The discussion will be dragged down to the level of its weakest partner, and stay stuck there, unless that person can step up to the level of emotional maturation which involves being tolerant of differences. The obvious question here is, *Where do I need to grow up in order to allow the one I love to be who he or she is?*

3) Our difficulty in sustaining ambiguity pushes us, consciously or unconsciously, toward manipulative behaviors designed to speed resolution or clarity. This is not bad in itself, but since the essential mystery of each person is finally an ambiguity, we are obliged to live it out over the long haul. As noted in an earlier chapter, the triple A's—ambiguity, ambivalence and anxiety—are omnipresent, especially in relationship. Our capacity to tolerate them is directly proportionate to our capacity to tolerate the reality of the other. Just as passion is incapable of being sustained

forever, so too the replacement emotions of disappointment, anger and resentment will claim their day as well. Again, the moral question is, *Where do I need to sustain, even suffer, ambiguity over the long haul, to allow the inherent truth of the relationship to emerge?*

For any relationship to survive, one needs luck, grace and patient devotion to dialogue. Luck because the world is replete with absurdities, variables, complexities, which have the power to destroy any of us anytime. We are in the hands of the capricious gods, whether we will or not, and much lies outside the control of even our best intentions. Grace obliges the strength of character which enables us to forgive ourselves and others for stupidity, cruelty, ignorance, narcissism and inattentiveness. As we and our partners are only fragile, frightened travelers, easily hurt and intimidated by the loud roar of the universe, we are all most needful of magnanimity of spirit. Touching, forgiving, accepting, comforting oneself and the other brings grace into this wounded world.

Patience is the necessary companion of grace. The work of relationship is never finished, vigilance never concluded, renewal never final. Patience means sticking something out because it is so important. Sometimes relationships must be ended because they are too wounded, too hurtful or hinder the individuation imperative, but relationships which still flicker with hope, resilience and purpose deserve fidelity and the commitment to show up and be accountable.

Hoping for luck and supplying patience and grace is a continuing task. And one may say as well, that addressing the heuristic questions of our own journey remains the chief way we can love the other, for thereby we become less of a burden. If the relationship is a candle in the surrounding dark, so we must also be aware that we inevitably carry that darkness into the relationship. William Stafford observed:

> It is important that awake people be awake. . . .
> The signals we give: yes, and no, or maybe should be clear.
> The darkness around us is deep.[115]

---

[115] "A Ritual To Read to Each Other," in *The Darkness Around Us Is Deep,* pp. 135f.

25
The Laughter of the Gods

Kierkegaard tells the story of the person who humbly petitioned the gods that he might, at the end of his life, have the last laugh. The gods sat solemnly, then slowly began to titter. The heavens shook with their laughter and he knew his petition had been granted.[116]

We are all aware of the tragic sense of life. Any mature person has discovered the truth of such a vision. Again, by "tragic" I refer not to terrible events but rather to a perception of the interplay of choice, chance, the gods and our own character, producing a web of consequences in which we are enmeshed. While we might lament those consequences and damn the gods, we are also in part responsible for them. What we chose in hubris and ignorance, now has come to us as crushing knowledge. What we did not know *did* prove to hurt us, and others.

But the mature sensibility must also leave place for the sense of absurdity, the belly laugh, the guffaw. Our word comedy comes from Latin *como,* village, suggesting its plebeian origins, even as the word tragedy derives from *tragos* plus *oda* (goat-song) of Dionysian religious rite. The comic sensibility is linked to the tragic sensibility, a spin-off of the same perception. Each observes and celebrates the fall of humanity. The classic comic pratfall is that of the inflated person slipping on a banana peel. What is that but a repeat of the Fall? We also find the humorous in the defeat of our expectations. Why did the rooster cross the road? To get to the other side. Why not? What is funny here?

Do you recall the story of two cannibals eating a clown and one of them asking, "Do you taste something funny?" What about the Dummling who expressed pride in solving a puzzle in only fifty days when it said "3-5 years" on the box cover? Or the one about the guy struggling across the desert who is approached by various individuals who have no water but seek to sell him a tie. He is incredulous at this and rejects their

---

[116] *Papers and Journals,* p. 138.

irrelevant offer. Finally, on his last legs, he arrives at the top of a hill and espies a beautiful oasis country club with freshets of water cascading everywhere. As he gratefully approaches this salvation, he is told: "Sir, you need a tie to come in." Or do you recall reversing the cassette on a country and western song where the guy gets his truck back, his dog back and his wife and kids back? Is something funny here?

When we see that our life has been filled with absurdity, with deflated arrogance, with leveling, humbling and educational reverses, then we may see that it is *La Comedie Humaine* after all. Laughter may provide some balance for all that grief. A funny thing happened on the way to the grave . . . it was my life. Just as mortality is the ultimate democracy, so we may say that comedy is the great equalizer. What dictator can withstand raillery and ridicule? Panzer tanks, yes, but the laughter of his foes, no. What ego inflation can withstand the awareness of our pretentious absurdity? If the grave is a leveler, so too is the comic sense of life.

And all this time we thought life was tragic and awful, and so it is, but it is also comic and laughable. We have mistaken ourselves even as we mistook Richard II for a king. In effect, we have all gone to a physician and said of our lives, "Doctor, when I touch my head with my finger it hurts. When I touch my knee it hurts. When I touch my chest it hurts." And he informs us that the problem is that we have a broken finger.

We have mistook our stories all these whiles. They really are funny. Our aspirations, our arrogance, our self-delusions, our inflations and expectations, all are part of a great balancing act performed by nature and the psyche. This balancing has at times a grave countenance and at others is wreathed in smiles. If one can bear to laugh at it, there is a blessing to be found in our comic journeys which partake of the godly vision. Don Quixote is a fool, a self-deluded, well-intended fool, as are we all, and yet he is worthy of our admiration as well as our laughter. He is no less blessed at the end of his journey, after much suffering, than is his brother Oedipus. Like Vladimir and Estragon, who wait for Godot, we are sojourners in a play whose lines and outcome are unpredictable. All we can say for sure is that we wait, fill the time in various ways, and wonder. If we are capable of laughing at our story, we may for a time visit the precincts of the godly—and have the last laugh.

26
Finding the Blue Light

When I was living in Zurich and devoting some years of my life to re-covering a sense of my true path, I experienced a number of synchronistic events. I had several dreams in which a blue light appeared. Then I stumbled across the Grimm fairy tale "The Blue Light." And soon after, as I stood on a balcony in Zollikon and looked down the Zurichsee at night, a blue light on the periphery of Zurich shimmered and seemed to embody all that which I had been seeking. It was a deeply compelling image. (Ultimately, I tracked down the light and found it was the sign of an insurance company, but that's another story.) So, the combination of this numinous light shimmering like the green light across the lake in Scott Fitzgerald's *The Great Gatsby* (an anima image if there ever was one), the appearance of the motif in several dreams, and the discovery of the Grimm tale, led me to consider this image as a symbol of the soul's journey. To this day, I have a blue glass mandala hanging in my window as a reminder.

While it is self-evident that large experiences shape us along the way, often distorting our vision and leading us down a road which was not intended for us, it is also clear that each of us has always had a blue light within. If we can understand it, it has an enormous role to play on our journey. Given the dependency inherent to our condition, we all defer that journey in favor of whatever our environment demands. It is our understandable identification with that adaptation which constitutes the false self, a provisional personality which may very well carry us through to the end of our days. But, in the end, it will not have been our life that we were living. It was the adapted life, not the one to which we were called. Over the decades, the slightest change in course will lead one many, many miles astray. We set sail for Cathay and wind up in Polynesia, and wonder how we got there. It was the uncorrected course, day after day, which lead us so far afield.

Friedrich Nietzsche said once that before one can find the path one first must have found the lantern.[117] That is his way of asking: "By what *lumen naturae,* light of nature, is our journey led?"

In "The Blue Light," a discharged soldier has fallen on hard times. We all have this experience periodically in the sense that the "king" we served, the dominant conscious values which direct our energies, no longer serves us. We experience a general loss of energy and sense of meaning, because from time to time the psyche protests the one-sidedness of our adaptation to life, the degree of deviation from our true course. Such symptoms are blessings in disguise; they are the psyche's way of getting our attention, summoning us to correct our course.

The itinerant soldier falls into the grip of a witch, symbolic of the negative anima experienced as depression. As is usually the case, he is obliged to be humbled, to work the earth and chop the wood, necessary means by which the old order is dismantled.

But then he is told to descend into a well, at the bottom of which burns a blue light which never goes out, and to return to the surface with it. When the witch wants him to surrender the blue light, he cannily refuses and in time is lead out of the depths by the assistance of a black dwarf. (A black dwarf had also appeared in my dreams, told me his name was Urgus and that he would help me. I knew his word was true and that he had numinous powers. His legs grew into the earth, so I knew his powers were chthonic and profound.)

The dwarf tells the soldier that whenever he is in need he must light his pipe with the blue light and the dwarf will appear to help. The dwarf represents the highly concentrated, often truncated, undeveloped powers which lie within each of us. We all have dwarfed energies, the acknowledgment and development of which will put immense resources at the disposal of conscious life. We sensed those powers as children, but found their public acknowledgment too costly, and so colluded over the years in their suppression. We ourselves dwarfed them.

With the help of the blue light, the *lumen naturae,* the soldier is able to employ the king's daughter in various tasks. That is to say, when a man is in contact with his authentic vision, his anima or spiritual side is

---

[117] *The Portable Nietzsche,* p. 48.

available to support the journey. The king, representing the old reigning order, the out-worn attitude of consciousness, resents this new energy and seeks to repress it. In like fashion, we all are our own worst enemies, resisting growth and change, opposing the developmental summons of the Self, seeking comfort within the old order even though it has led to depression.

The king throws the soldier into prison but the soldier is again rescued by the power which comes from lighting his pipe at the blue light. This tells us that when we are able to reconnect with our guiding vision, even the powers of collectivity must yield.

When we look at the structure of "The Blue Light," we see first that the soldier is an energy no longer valued by the attitudes of consciousness. Rejected by the king, the energy falls into the grip of the witch. But, as those who have worked on themselves know, at the bottom of the well of depression there is always some meaningful task. *Depression is life pressed down*. When one can find that vital connection once again, the natural energy and purposiveness returns and the depression lifts. Periodic depressions are common and natural, as the psyche seeks the cooperation of consciousness to alter its course along new channels of expression.

So the soldier energy, once valued, bounces from king to witch, but at the bottom of the well of depression is the inner light that empowers one to reenter life. Contact with the dwarf allows access to repressed psychic energies. The combination of the illumination, the vision and the powers of the psyche make him a considerable presence in the world. When one's contact with the natural light is secure, the anima is supportive, the old order cedes its sovereignty and the soldier becomes the new king.

The paradigm of this process is instructive to us all. We each have our natural light, an image of what our soul intends for us. For some of us it was clear in the beginning of life, for others it is discovered along the way. And for many to whom it was once clear, it must be rediscovered after diverse directional errors. Because the message of our powerlessness is often overlearned, we are all, to some extent, conditioned away from our blue light. The symptomatology we are often able to suppress in the first half of life breaks through in a kind of divine insurgency in the second half. Before we can begin to question our adaptation, we usually need to become miserable. This is where therapy, or some analogous form of disciplined dialogue, can be helpful.

If the reader reflects honestly on his or her earliest visions, preoccupations and hopes, chances are he or she will reconnect with that blue light. For me certain lines of Yeats summon up what my life, for all its peregrinations and wrong turnings, has been about; for instance:

> Those images that yet
> Fresh images beget,
> That dolphin-torn, that gong-tormented sea.[118]

Byzantium was a symbol of Yeats's own spiritual quest. In my case, I have felt since childhood that my personal task was to sail on what I imaged as a "Devil-torn, God-tormented sea." In my early years the heart had its attachments to such a journey, and served me best in encounters with the mystery of nature and in the field of imaginative play. As a young adult, I followed the life of the mind and the study of theology, philosophy and spirituality. After a fall into the well at midlife, I discovered that Jungian psychology provided a blue light which could illumine not only the recesses of the well, but much of the natural world as well. As a result, though I still sail a Devil-torn, God-tormented sea, I feel blessed to have seen that blue light shining at the end of the Zurichsee.

Underneath the surface of our lives, that natural vision and personal urgency has always been at work. Sometimes we can discern its intentions and align our conscious choices with it, but most of the time it languishes like a light shining at the bottom of a well, into which no one would venture unless absolutely necessary. We do not choose this light; it seeks us, and always has. If one reflects on the core interests and aspirations of one's life, scattered as they may be by the vicissitudes of fate, the intervention of forces over which we had little control, as well as the collusive choices of our own Quisling ego, one does still, intuitively, know what one's life is about. It will be different for each of us; even when the themes are the same, the paths will vary.

---

[118] "Byzantium," in *Selected Poems and Two Plays,* p. 133.

There is no clear path across that sea, but the blue light shines on its furthest shore, always has, and still summons each of us to it. Finding and following one's blue light, with whatever resources are available to us as adults, helps us recover what the child intuited but was unable to enact at the time. The recovery of one's personal blue light is essential for the discovery of purpose and depth in the second half of life. It is always there, awaiting our arrival.

PART THREE

Being Here

Let everyone mind his own business, and endeavor
to be what he was made.
—Thoreau, *Walden.*

27
Gratitude

It is easy enough to whine, to lament one's state, to wish things otherwise. No doubt we have all done so in the face of life's unfairness and the dashing of our dreams. Behind this lament is the fantasy that there is something which is *supposed* to happen, that what we wish is somehow necessary, important and inevitable. The inherent narcissism of our condition is truly hard to overthrow, despite life's repeated battering of our grandiosity.

Nevertheless, I deeply believe that one ought to spend some part of every day of the second half of life in a profound gratitude. I do. Some have thought my books pessimistic, even depressive, even as others found hope in them. I am of the latter school of thought. Such hope comes from the capacity of the individual to take on his or her life, gain some purchase on selfhood and find deeper meaning. That possibility, however daunting, is energizing to me amid all the depressive moments of life.

So, let us pause for a moment to be grateful, before asking in a final chapter, "Where are we?"

Anyone reading this book is privileged to be above ground rather than pushing daisies. My best friend in college died in a car crash one year after we graduated. He was by far the better man. My life has been a loan ever since. Anyone reading this book is privileged to live in the twentieth century with its unprecedented possibilities of choice and learning, including the insights of depth psychology. Even our most recent ancestors had none of these.

Though our Western culture is cursed by trivial pursuits, rampant consumerism and reductive ideologies, no previous era has provided individuals with a wider spectrum of possibilities. When Jung observed that the modern fell off the roof of the medieval cathedral,[119] he was acknowl-

---

[119] *Letters,* vol. 2, p. 569.

edging the crisis of meaning which has fallen upon us. The good news, however, is that humanity has never been freer to choose its values. Rather than lament the loss of a stabilizing tribal mythology, the good old days, the way things were, we all need to be grateful for the fact that we are relatively freer to find, affirm and live our values than were those at any other time in history. Freedoms that we absolutely take for granted were not available even to our parents. One millennium ago, half the population of Europe died before age five. Life expectancy in the Western world averaged only 47 in 1900, now it is over 70.

It is to our shame that we whine about the hard blows of life when our lives are so much more comfortable than ever before, and so many of us are privileged to have those additional years in which to recover the journey of the soul.

Rather than say, "I have to go to work," feeling that our work life is a burden, we might better acknowledge the privilege of being productive, of being able to contribute to the support of our loved ones. And if we don't feel productive, we can change our work. Rather than say, "I have to . . ." let us decide what in fact we do have to do and what we don't, and be grateful that we have a choice.

Earlier this day I met with a man in his mid-thirties who has been professionally successful but who suffers from depression. He feels trapped by his work. When I asked him what he really wanted to do, he said, "Take a year off to find out." When I suggested that such a step was possible, he said, "Oh, but I couldn't do that." I suggested that he could, but that he was not willing to face the consequences of his choice. To choose to so value his life's journey as to pull out of it to consider the right course would cause suffering, but not to do so would also cause suffering. Which was the more meaningful suffering? While not suggesting that what was right for one person would be right for another, I related that I had faced a similar dilemma, taken a leave, and lived for thirteen months with my family in a foreign country—begging, borrowing and metaphorically stealing to make it possible. And, terrifying as that choice was, it was the right thing to do because it was choosing to take the agenda of my soul seriously.

So, we all have choices. Is life difficult, unfair, complex, labyrinthine, never without painful consequences? It has always been that way, and worse. The good news is that we have choices, that never in human history has the collective had less authority to usurp the soul, and that your life lies before you as possibility. Even with all the diminishments of chronic pain, with which I for one daily live, with aging, with which we all live until we do not live, and with the terribly powerful regressive forces within us, we all still have the choice to grow or decline, enlarge or diminish, take life on or retreat from it.

Soberly, realistically, let us be grateful for the considerable blessing which the loss of tribal mythology brings us; for the small advantage that depth psychology brings us; and for the enormous potential that the loss of collective meaning brings us by obliging us to create our own meaning. Through risk and suffering we may at last come upon those values which bring resonant assent from deep within. Then we have created a life worthy of the soul.

28
So, Where Are We, Then?

> Imagination eludes the determinations of psychology . . . . and consti-
> tutes an autochthonous, autogenous realm. We subscribe to this view:
> rather than the will, rather than the *élan vital*, imagination is the true
> source of psychic production. Psychically, we are created by our rev-
> erie—created and limited by our reverie—for it is the reverie which
> delineates the furthest limits of our mind.
> —Gaston Bachelard, *The Psychoanalysis of Fire.*

As Bachelard suggests above, and as Jung also insisted, we are all and
always in thrall to images, whether culturally imposed, complex-driven
or consciously chosen. Any fantasy about creating a life, or that *this one*
might *be* our life, will depend on those images, and the values they embody, to which we have given ourselves. It is essential to be realistic
about such mythological images and their effect in our lives. If we do not
consciously endorse their values, then we are living someone else's
myth, or sleeping our way through ours. Either one chooses such imagos,
namely "value-dynamic images," or they are someone else's choice. As
powerful as the will is, as urgent and insistent the *élan vital,* the imagination creates the world in which we live. The only question is: whose
imagination, whose images, whose myth are we living in the course of
that which we call our life?

I have sought here to honestly represent the immense difficulty of creating a life. The naiveté of youth must be replaced with a rich apprecia-
tion of the challenge. The tendency of the so-called New Age folks is to
finesse this difficulty and look to external gurus and magical thinking for
help. It is not that simple, as most of us know. The difficulties of creating
a life are compounded by the power of the unconscious, early condition-
ing and the fragility of our consciousness and will. Yet, the whole purpose and dignity of our lives is directly proportionate to the degree that
one takes on this great labyrinthine puzzle in the second half of life. The

first half of life is usually a gigantic, unavoidable mistake. But the second half gives us another shot at it, after all the wounds from which we learn, after the buffeting of the ego which strengthens consciousness, after all the hard-learned lessons which prove to be invaluable.

Each of us may find our paradigm in Oedipus, who was thrown into a life full of omens and probabilities, determinations and limitations—just like us. He fled those omens and walked right into their fulfillment—as have we. He had three appointments—as do we. His first appointment was the summons into a finite life, a birth fraught with unlimited potential yet everywhere bounded by invisible limits. The second appointment was to arrive at Thebes, full of himself, convinced he knew who he was. We, too, have all been there. And, like Oedipus, we have all suffered the undoing which leads us to the knowledge that we don't really know ourselves after all. The third appointment was the one that Sophocles, allegedly in his ninetieth year, insisted that Oedipus keep—the appointment at Colonus.

After Thebes, after the stunning humiliation of midlife, Oedipus spends his final years in humble wandering, wondering what it is that the gods wish him to know. He learns, he absorbs, he winds his weary exile to Colonus, where he is blessed by the gods for the sincerity of his journey. It was not so much that he created his life, as that he allowed at last that life might create him, as the gods had intended. The price of this gift, both precious and perilous, was exile and suffering; the price of not finding his calling was ignorance, pettiness and annihilation of the soul.

Oedipus is our finest paradigm because he kept his appointments. We were all thrust into a world of givens. Each of us has already been to Thebes, the life realized according to the dictates of the collective, reinforced by the inflated, delusional consciousness of early adulthood. But each of us still has an appointment at Colonus. Will we keep it? After years of exile and suffering, rich with the wisdom which is the gift of such a journey, we may at last come to our personal Colonus, the life the gods intended us to have, the place where life creates us.

So, where are we then? On which road, the one that forever circles back to Thebes, or the one which leads to an unknown place, the place where we may meet the meaning of our journey?

Bibliography

Adams, Hazard, ed. *Critical Theory Since Plato.* New York: Harcourt, Brace, Jovanovich, Inc., 1970.

Adler, Gerhard, "Aspects of Jung's Personality." In *Psychological Perspectives,* vol. 6, no. 1 (Spring 1975).

Alighieri, Dante. *The Comedy of Dante Alighieri.* Trans. Dorothy Sayers. New York: Basic Books, 1963.

Anderson, Walter Truett, ed. *The Truth About the Truth.* New York: Jeremy P. Tarcher/Putnam Books, 1995.

Aristotle. *Poetics.* Ed. and Trans. Francis Ferguson. New York: Hill and Wang, 1961.

Bachelard, Gaston. *The Psychoanalysis of Fire.* Trans. Alan C. Ross. Boston: Beacon Press, 1964.

Bonhoeffer, Dietrich. *Letters and Papers from Prison.* New York: MacMillan, 1972.

Calosso, Robert. *Ka.* New York: Alfred A. Knopf, 1998.

Camus, Albert. *The Fall.* Trans. Justin O'Brien. New York: Vintage Books, 1956.

_____. *The Myth of Sisyphus.* Trans. Justin O'Brien. New York: Alfred A. Knopf, 1955.

Cavafy, Constantin. *The Complete Poems of Cavafy.* Trans. Rae Dalven. New York: Harvest Books, 1961.

Chapman, Richard C., and Gavrin, Jonathan. "Suffering: The Contribution of Persistent Pain." In *The Lancet,* vol. 353 (June 26, 1999).

Eliot, T.S. *The Complete Poems and Plays of T.S. Eliot.* New York: Harcourt, Brace and World, 1952.

Ellmann, Richard, and O'Clair, Robert. *Modern Poems: An Introduction to Poetry.* New York: W.W. Norton and Co., 1976.

Fowles, John. *The French Lieutenant's Woman.* New York: New American Library, 1969.

Freud, Sigmund. *The Psychopathology of Everyday Life.* New York: W.W. Norton and Co., 1971.

Hillman, James. *The Soul's Code: In Search of Character and Calling.* New York: Warner Books, 1996.

Hirsch, Edward. *On Love*. New York: Alfred A. Knopf, 1998.

Hollis, James. *The Eden Project: In Search of the Magical Other*. Toronto: Inner City Books, 1998.

_____. *The Middle Passage: From Misery to Meaning in Midlife*. Toronto: Inner City Books, 1993.

_____. *Swamplands of the Soul: New Life in Dismal Places*. Toronto: Inner City Books, 1996.

_____. *Tracking the Gods: The Place of Myth in Modern Life*. Toronto: Inner City Books, 1995.

_____. *Under Saturn's Shadow: The Wounding and Healing of Men*. Toronto: Inner City Books, 1994.

Homer, *War Songs*. Trans. Christopher Logue. New York: Noonday Press, 1997.

Hopkins, Gerard Manley. *A Hopkins Reader*. Ed. John Pick. New York: Doubleday, 1966.

James, Williams. *Varieties of Religious Experience*. New York: Mentor, 1958.

Joyce, James. *The Dubliners*. New York: Modern Library, 1954.

Jung, C.G. *The Collected Works*. (Bollingen Series XX). 20 vols. Trans. R.F.C. Hull, Ed. H. Read, M. Fordham, G. Adler, Wm. McGuire. Princeton: Princeton University Press, 1973.

_____. *Letters*. (Bollingen Series XCV), 2 vols. Princeton: Princeton University Press, 1973.

_____. *Nietzsche's* Zarathustra: *Notes of the Seminar Given in 1934-1939* (Bollingen Series XCIX). 2 vols. Ed. James L. Jarrett. Princeton University Press, 1988.

Kazantzakis, Nikos. *The Last Temptation of Christ*. New York: Simon and Schuster, 1960.

Kierkegaard, Søren. *Papers and Journals: A Selection*. Trans. Alastar Hannay, London: Penguin Books, 1996.

Lawrence, D.H. *Sons and Lovers*. New York: Viking Press, 1913.

Maddox, Brenda. *D.H. Lawrence: the Story of a Marriage*. New York: Simon and Schuster, 1994.

Maloney, Mercedes, and Maloney, Anne. *The Hand That Rocks the Cradle*. Englewood Cliffs, NJ: Prentice-Hall, 1985.

Milton, John. *The Complete Poems*. Ed. John Leonard. New York: Penguin, 1999.

Nietzsche, Friedrich. *The Portable Nietzsche.* Trans. Walter Kaufmann. New York: Viking Press, 1968.

Oliver, Mary. *New and Selected Poems.* Boston: Beacon Press, 1992.

Pascal, Blaise. *Pensées.* Trans. A.J. Krailsheimer. New York: Penguin Books, 1995.

Prater, Donald. *A Ringing Glass: The Life of Rainer Maria Rilke.* Oxford: Oxford University Press, 1986.

Rilke, Rainer Maria. *Letters of Rainer Maria Rilke.* Trans. Jane Green and M.D. Herter Norton. New York: W.W. Norton and Co., 1972.

_____. *Letters to a Young Poet.* Trans. M.D. Herter Norton. New York: W.W. Norton and Co., 1962.

Sartre, Jean-Paul. *Existentialism and Humanism.* London: Methuen, 1948.

Sharp, Daryl. *Jungian Psychology Unplugged: My Life As an Elephant.* Toronto: Inner City Books, 1998.

Stafford, William. *The Darkness Around Us Is Deep: Selected Poems of William Stafford.* Ed. Robert Bly. New York: Harper, 1993.

Thoreau, Henry David. *Walden, Or, Life in the Woods.* Boston: Shambhala, 1992.

Tillich, Paul. *Theology of Culture.* Oxford: Oxford University Press, 1959.

Untermeyer, Louis, ed. *A Concise Treasury of Great Poems.* New York: Simon and Schuster, 1942.

Vaughan-Lee, Llewellyn. *Sufism: The Transformation of the Heart.* Inverness, CA: The Golden Sufi Center, 1995.

Willey, Basil. *Nineteenth Century Studies: Coleridge to Matthew Arnold.* New York: Harper, 1966.

Yeats, W.B. *Selected Poems and Two Plays.* Ed. M.L. Rosenthal. New York: MacMillan, 1962.

Index

Studies in Jungian Psychology
by Jungian Analysts

Quality Paperbacks